John Pritchard was Bishop of Oxf___
He was formerly Bishop of J_
Canterbury. He has served in _
and was Warden of Cranmer H_
than twenty books, including _T_
Again on the Christian Journey, _____ _Your_
Faith, The Life and Work of a Prie. _____us, God Lost and Found,_
Living Faithfully, Ten, Something More and _Five Events that Made_
Christianity.

HANDBOOK OF CHRISTIAN MINISTRY

For lay and ordained Christians

John Pritchard

First published in Great Britain in 2020

Society for Promoting Christian Knowledge
36 Causton Street
London SW1P 4ST
www.spck.org.uk

British Library Cataloguing-in-Publication Data
A catalogue record for this book is available from the British Library

ISBN 978–0–281–08439–5
eBook ISBN 978–0–281–08440–1

Typeset by Fakenham Prepress Solutions, Fakenham, Norfolk NR21 8NL
First printed in Great Britain by Ashford Colour Press
Subsequently digitally reprinted in Great Britain

eBook by Fakenham Prepress Solutions, Fakenham, Norfolk NR21 8NL

Produced on paper from sustainable forests

Contents

Acknowledgements

In the short term this book has benefited from the help of several people – the huge wisdom of Gordon Oliver, the kind encouragement of Gillian Lunn, the loving scrutiny of my wife Wendy and, as always, the guidance and skill of Alison Barr, my faithful editor for many years and many books.

In the longer term, however, the book comes out of the patient practise of ministry that I've been privileged to observe and to share in the parish of Wilton in Taunton, among some fine cohorts of ordinands at Cranmer Hall, and in parishes in the dioceses of Canterbury, Durham and Oxford.

As a final source of inspiration, I want to pay tribute to friends at St Mary's Church, Richmond, in North Yorkshire, where it's now my pleasure to worship and share in ministry. It is to them that I dedicate this book.

A word at the beginning

It's been said that nothing important comes with instructions. Love, courage, mercy, compassion, forgiveness, and more, must come under that heading. But what about ministry? Are there instructions to be followed there?

Again, I think not. Ministry is too personal, too varied and too eccentric to be guided by a book of instructions. So this is not a book of instructions. Nor is it attempting to be a definitive or comprehensive manual. Nor is it a book of hints and tips (although I do rather like the suggestions Dallas Willard made to a young man who was going into ministry and asked for advice. He said, 'One: ruthlessly eliminate rush. And two: spend the next twenty years reading the Gospels.').

This is a book of principles and ideas. It's a series of headlines. It makes suggestions and offers invitations. I hope that it will be useful. And it's for every Christian, not just those with authorized ministries. We have to set God's people free because all of us have a calling to minister God's grace in some way or other. Ministry is one of those code words that are much used but often unexplained. I take it that ministry is how the Church, through its people, expresses and embodies God's love for the world. It's the call to serve after the pattern of Jesus and it's a calling conferred on all Christians through baptism. We're all in this together.

Inevitably, it's a personal A–Z because it's written by one person out of his experience of ministry. I realize it's a risky venture to write on a subject about which every reader will have strong views. We all, lay and ordained Christians, care deeply about our calling and getting it right and doing it better. Writing about ministry is a bit like writing about humility – how can anyone be bold enough to write about *that*?

But here it is: a handbook of Christian ministry, which I've dared to write for two reasons. First, because I think of it as a companion volume to *The Life and Work of a Priest*,[1] which seems to have been appreciated by a fair number of people. Second, because I've loved my experience of ministry – every year of it – and I've had a good number of roles through which to see how ministry operates in the Church. I've seen the golden blaze of 'successful' ministry and I've seen ministry sadly diminished. I've admired the poetry of quiet faith and the patience of attentive listening. I've watched the smoke of disappointment drifting over a ministry and the secret sadness of hope left in ruins. I've seen ministry that's been beautiful, warm and attractive, and ministry that's been hard-edged and self-obsessed. In this handbook, I've wanted to offer a few lessons learnt through all of this. Yes, it's unavoidably partial and personal, but it is, nevertheless, born of experience and deep affection for those with whom I've shared the journey.

Who is it for? It's for those who see that part of their life as a Christian involves ministry with and to others, which I hope means those with any intention of taking their faith seriously. All of us are called to ministry by the privilege of baptism. I met a wonderful 78-year-old living up Swaledale who had never lived more than a hundred yards from the church he'd served faithfully in any number of ways all his life. If he's interested, it's for him. It's also for a priest in the middle of a hectic ministry who just wants to step back for a moment and think again about what she's doing in a particular area of her ministry. If she comes across this book, it's for her too. It's for the hard-pressed churchwarden and the faithful homegroup leader. It's for the pastoral visitor and the Children and Families Worker. It's for any Christian, because all are called.

Jesus involved several circles of friends in his ministry (and all our ministry is, first of all, *his* ministry). There were three friends who got the closest inside view. There were twelve who walked alongside and did their best, though they often fluffed it. There were several astonishing women who did much of the financial and emotional heavy lifting right to the end. There were seventy who set off boldly with a prayer, a message and half a sandwich.

There were doubtless many others in the crowds who listened and marvelled and took up the challenge to make love their priority.

Ministry is a big tent. This handbook is for lay and ordained Christians wanting to make the most of the ministries God has called them into.

I've taken the A–Z shape simply to control the territory. You'll notice that there's not much on 'Z', but there are two entries for 'C', 'P' and 'S'. It may be inconsistent, but how can you *not* have both Care *and* Children, Prayer *and* Preaching, or Self-care *and* Suffering? It goes without saying that this book doesn't need to be read all the way through; it's one to dip into as interest suggests.

Whatever I write, I try to make accessible and, in the best sense, useful. For those who want to go further and deeper, there exists now a wonderful book *The Study of Ministry*, edited by Martyn Percy, which provides a comprehensive survey of theory and best practice in ministry.[2] That book has a feast of articles by leading theologians and practitioners. My aim is more modest. I want to help the hard-pressed yet highly motivated Christians who shine like stars throughout the Church, but don't want or need anything too detailed. I've tried as well not to be too denominational, but my background is hard to disguise.

We minister in interesting times. So much is in flux, including our way of understanding our Christian faith. Brian McLaren has written widely on the changes as he sees them:

> For centuries, Christianity has been presented as a system of beliefs, [and] that system of beliefs has supported a wide range of unintended consequences. What would it mean for Christians to rediscover their faith not as a problematic system of beliefs but as a just and generous way of life, rooted in contemplation and expressed in compassion? Could Christians migrate from defining their faith as a system of beliefs to expressing it as a loving way of life?[3]

That's a major shift, but it has at its heart the place where belief and practice meet, and that's in the priority of love. A liberating emphasis on love was the hallmark of Jesus' ministry – for God, for self, for neighbour, for stranger, for outcast, for enemy. Love decentred everything else; it relativized everything else. Love took priority over everything.

It does this for us in our ministries today. Love is its meaning.

A

Attentiveness

The heart of Christian ministry is attentiveness. This is absolutely central. If we give our focused attention to God, to others, to our context and to ourselves, then we stand a good chance of doing the Christlike thing in the situations we're facing.

It might be a problem of today (though it's more likely to be a perennial human failing) that we so often seem to be careless, unfocused and unobservant in the way we go through life, shimmying around problems, seeking easy answers, absorbed in our own world. Attentiveness, by contrast, is a habit, a discipline that keeps us alert to where God is and how God is present in any and every situation. Let's look at the dimensions of this attentiveness.

Attentiveness to God

Being attentive means living in the compassionate gaze of God who forever reaches out to us in love, desiring our response. This releases us from our constant self-absorption and judgement of ourselves. When we turn away from self, we find our reference point and purpose in God and in the reign of God that's in bud all around us. We simply want to return that loving gaze, that attentiveness, every day. It's a bit like the sunflower that lives constantly in the gaze of the sun and responds by following the sun throughout the day as it crosses the sky. Why? Because it draws its life from the sun, just as we draw our life from the gaze of God.

In our ministries, we encounter great joys and equally great disappointments. Sometimes the romance of faith is all-embracing; sometimes we're caught in a gridlock of sterile arguments; sometimes we live with an avalanche of sorrows. Only by being held in the secure, graceful hands of God can we be sure of having the resilience we need. Hopefully, we will never let the disappointments of ministry hide from our sight the beauty of God and the joy of resurrection.

That is why prayer is the essential starting point for ministry. Ministry is the overflow of our life in God, and so it depends on how seriously we attend to the love that forever flows towards us from the Trinity. We seek only to catch a fraction of that divine energy so we can pass it on and be a conduit of God's love to the world. In this way, we start our day seeking God, putting ourselves in the way of God and opening our lives to God's grace. St John of the Cross wrote, 'God is up early and waiting to shine upon us, if only we will open the curtains.'[1]

So, making time and space for these life-giving encounters with God is our first priority, and that means some pretty serious slowing down of our lives. Much of life today seems to involve racing from one place or one task to another, focused intently on where we're going rather than on where we are. But it's where we are that matters, because that is where life is, and if life is there, so is God. God comes to us in the heart of life. We can't meet God in yesterday's activities or in tomorrow's, only in today's, only in the fascinating succession of 'nows'.

Most of us learn this the hard way. 'I know you're very busy, but . . . ', says the person wanting to talk. 'It'll only take a moment,' she says. 'I'm sorry to interrupt,' he begins (little realizing that it's often in the interruptions that our most important ministry lies). What we should probably hear is that we're giving the impression of being so busy that we're racing past people's needs and they don't want to bother us. We can then neither meet the person, nor the God who has brought that person to us. God is a three-mile-an-hour God, said one theologian; that's the speed at which the love of God walks.[2]

If God is the frame of reference for how we live each day, we stand a better chance of recognizing God's fingerprints and responding faithfully. Attentiveness to God always comes first.

Quick idea: the square yard

One helpful exercise in attentiveness is to focus for twenty minutes on a square yard of the natural world, ideally by water, though a back garden will do fine. Sit by the square yard and notice the things you're never ordinarily aware of – the shape and texture of the stones, the tiny insects scurrying around, the wispy spiders' webs, the light dancing on the water, the different shades of green in the grasses and leaves, and the way water makes different shapes every time it moves over rocks. It might look messy at first, but could we improve it? No chance. After a while, this attentiveness leads to respect, and respect leads to reverence, and reverence leads to joyful thanks to the Creator who's behind such intricate beauty and delicate diversity. That square yard becomes sacred ground, but the secret is in the looking and the staying.

Attentiveness to others

God inhabits the present moment and that's really the only place we can experience God and be captivated by the divine gaze. It follows that, if we are to be agents of God's love, we will need to be unconditionally attentive to the people God sets before us. You could say that attentiveness to others is the beginning and end of pastoral care.

Simone Weil, French philosopher and mystic, said, 'Attention is the rarest and purest form of generosity.'[3] It's rare because the 'drinks party experience' is so common. You're at a party and talking to someone, but that person is clearly not very interested in the conversation, constantly looking over your shoulder to see if there's someone more interesting to talk to. It is demoralizing and demeaning, and can leave you feeling humiliated and angry.

Barbara Brown Taylor puts it neatly when she writes:

The point is to see the person standing right in front of me [as someone who] has no substitute, who can never be replaced, whose heart holds things for which there is no language, whose life is an unsolved mystery. The moment I turn that person into a character in my own story, the encounter is over. I have stopped being a human being and have become a fiction writer instead.[4]

It's so obvious, but also so rare. Every Christian – indeed every person who manages to give this attentiveness to another – will have known the gratitude of someone saying that talking to us has been wonderfully helpful, even though we know that all we did was to attend closely and listen. What we're doing, of course, is giving ourselves unconditionally as one human being to another. It means keeping genuine eye contact (not a dead eye – it shows), listening with all of our body and being alert and responsive to any signals of distress. We're listening and attending to the bass line, not just the melody.

The person before us is the only person we are with at that moment and deserves our full attention. That person is made in the image of God and, therefore, is of absolute value. It surely isn't impossible to make ourselves fully available to that person in the time we're with them, and then to do the same with the next person. This moment will not come again. It's precious.

Attentiveness to our context

Sadly, it's possible to be so concerned with the activities of our churches that we live in a religious bubble, without relating to the community's real existence, its joys and struggles. The Church is a jealous mistress and will always take as much of our time as we're prepared to give. We have to remember that 'God so loved *the world* that he gave his only Son' (John 3.16), not that he so loved the church council and the Christmas fayre.

We need, therefore, to be attentive to the community around us if we are not to be a religious club for those who like that sort of thing. Do we understand what's going on around us? Are we genuinely interested in it? Do we think of it as God's beloved place of residence or just as a pond to fish in? It's sometimes hard for us really to take in that the flourishing of the 95 per cent of people who don't regularly come to church is just as much God's concern as the spiritual growth of those inside the doors on Sundays. God isn't proud, and he doesn't have favourites. Look at all the people you meet on the street, in the supermarket, in the gym or the pub and remember that God loves them just as much as God loves you. It's a humbling experience.

To attend to our context means identifying the focal points in the community where people gather. Do they gather around schools, clubs, community choirs, civic societies, charity groups or elsewhere? How can we engage with those activities? Is there a way that Christians can help these groups to fulfil their best purposes? What are the issues that concern local people? Are they being addressed and how can the church help? Are there particular gaps in local provision that your church could meet? How does the community celebrate its existence and its uniqueness? A church can often act as a focus and facilitator for such celebrations, just as it can often help a community lament its tragedies.

In other words, how can your church be a blessing to the community? Above all, is your church a community of grace and good news? These are good questions for the church council, and ones that don't automatically present themselves in church life. They need intentionality from those who want to help their church fulfil its calling to be an agent of transformation in every part of life. God's purpose is 'to gather up all things in him [Christ], things in heaven *and things on earth*' (Ephesians 1.10). The vision is cosmic, a healed and renewed creation, glimpsed in embryo in the risen Christ and in his embodying of a new world. To limit ourselves to the walls and worries of a church is to miss the Big Idea – the reign of God in every part of life.

Attentiveness to ourselves

If we are to offer this attentiveness to God, to others and to the context we're in, we have to be attentive to our own well-being. Because ministry is often fuelled by guilt as well as faithful idealism, we can easily lose the joy or succumb to stress. This is a many-sided issue and is tackled in the chapter on **Self-care**.

Tailpiece: the Pope's blessing

Pope Francis was on a flight to South America for a papal visit. Carlos, one of the flight attendants, approached him as they flew over the Andes and asked him if he would bless his marriage to Paula, who was also on the plane as a flight attendant. The Pope listened to their story of how they had intended to marry in church years ago but, on the very day of their wedding, an earthquake had hit their village and destroyed the church. Sadly, they had never got back to organizing a church wedding and now they were ten years on and had two much-loved daughters.

Pope Francis not only agreed to bless their marriage but offered them a full marriage, there and then. Of course, there were many objections that could have been made to this gracious offer. There was no paperwork; there had been no investigations, no confession and no liturgical propriety. But all of that counted as nothing to the Pope as he married them (or blessed their marrying each other). The Pope knew that sacraments are for people, rather than people being there for the sacraments. There was rejoicing in the plane that day, and surely rejoicing in heaven.

The Pope was attentive to God (what would Jesus do?) He was attentive to the couple (what do they need for fulfilment and joy?) He was attentive to the situation (this is unusual but I may never see them again). He ministered God's love.

But maybe you can only do this if you're the Pope?

Resources

Barbara Brown Taylor, *The Preaching Life: Living out your vocation* (Norwich: Canterbury Press, 2013).

Judy Hirst, *Struggling to be Holy* (London: Darton, Longman & Todd, 2006).

Eugene H. Peterson, *Under the Unpredictable Plant: An exploration in vocational holiness* (Leominster: Gracewing, 1992).

Ronald Rolheiser, *Sacred Fire: A vision for a deeper human and Christian maturity* (New York: Image, 2014).

Samuel Wells, *Incarnational Ministry: Being with the Church* (Norwich: Canterbury Press, 2017).

B

Bible

When the sovereign is given a copy of the Bible at his or her coronation, it's with the words, 'We present you with this book, the most valuable thing that this world affords. Here is wisdom; this is the royal law. These are the lively oracles of God.'

It's a far cry from how most people in our culture see the Bible. The Bible is a bit like a telescope – if we look *through* it, we see worlds beyond, but if we merely look *at* it, we see only another object. It takes someone from outside our faith tradition to spell out what we're missing. Gandhi said:

> You Christians look after a document containing enough dynamite to blow all civilisations to pieces, turn the world upside down, and bring peace to a battle-torn planet. But you treat it as though it is nothing more than a piece of literature.[1]

For those involved in Christian ministry, the Bible is our inspiration, guidebook, resource and delight. But it has to be handled with intelligence because it's also a complicated document, open to misunderstanding or, at worst, abuse.

What is the Bible?

It's a library The Bible contains 66 books, written and compiled over a thousand years. It's a record of the Jewish and Christian understanding of God as it both changed and remained consistent during all those years. Certain passages written in earlier periods have to be seen as being 'of their time', but it's the consistencies that are most striking.

It's a book of words about the Word As we read the Bible, we find it converges on Jesus, then explodes again to shower the world with grace. But the contents are radically diverse. Rowan Williams, the former Archbishop of Canterbury, likens this diversity to a book that contains within the same two covers 'Shakespeare's sonnets, the law reports of 1910, the introduction to Kant's *Critique of Pure Reason*, the letters of St Anselm and a fragment of *The Canterbury Tales*'.[2] The Bible has a kaleidoscope of genres, but at its centre is the commanding figure of Jesus.

It's a love story It tells how God has sought and found his beloved people, who always wanted to go their own way and paid the price in great unhappiness. The Divine Lover who called out in the Garden, 'Adam, where are you?' continued that search right through to an Easter garden where a new world was born.

It's a conversation between friends You love and respect friends, you enjoy them and spend rewarding times with them. You don't expect always to agree with them; sometimes you might even argue with them. But you trust them to tell you the truth. On a grander scale, you might even say that the Bible is a conversation between heaven and earth, to which we're invited to listen, share and respond.

It's a book initiated and inspired by God but written by fallible humans It's a symphony of divinely inspired human voices bearing witness to our growing understanding of God. The many writers of the Bible didn't just take down God's dictation. Their work reveals the limitations and preconceptions of their time but, crucially, it bears witness to the transformational experience of their encounters with God. The writers invite us into this experience for ourselves, as do Christians when we introduce the Bible to others.

It's a radical, unsettling text as well as a book of beauty and inspiration Christians started off reading the Bible as subversive literature when the Church was under pressure and persecution, but later started reading it as a kind of establishment literature, suitable for a Church with power and privilege. This was a dangerous move. It domesticated the Bible and encouraged Christians to see it as an encyclopaedia of moral truths instead of a narrative of God's revolutionary love working through history.

What is the Bible? It's a love story that culminates in the great disclosure of the kingdom of God bursting into the world in the person of Jesus.

Approaching the text of the Bible

What we often find in ministry is that people don't know how to get into the Bible. They may, at some idealistic stage, have tried to read through it, starting at Genesis, only to grind to a halt somewhere in the complexities of Leviticus. They may hear it read in church in small fragments but regret that the bloodletting of some of the wilder parts of the Old Testament is left unexplained. They may encounter others who often say 'the Bible says,' and feel guilty for not knowing for themselves what the Bible says. It all adds up to the Bible seeming like a foreign country, best left to professional explorers or religious geeks.

Here are three ways to help people think about the text of Scripture.

1 What, why, how?

We ask first *what* the passage is actually about. Who is saying what to whom and why? Who else is around and what are they doing? Where is this happening, and how does it relate to what has just gone before and what comes after?

We then ask *why* is this passage here, and why is it saying what it does? What's going on behind the scenes? Why has the author written this, and what would the first readers and hearers have made of it?

Finally, we ask *how* does this passage apply to the world we know? How does the wisdom of the story work out in our context? What does it have to say to the wider world we inhabit today?

2 Text and context

The text itself What is the text saying? What kind of material is this – history, poetry, wisdom, law, prayer, prophecy? This isn't a one-dimensional book and each part must be read within its own genre.

The context What's the social world behind the text? What are the religious practices, the customs, the politics and the economic relationships? Where does the power lie? This is where particular scholars and parts of the Internet yield fascinating background (see 'Resources' below).

The subtext What is the author's purpose in writing this and in this way? What's the guiding theology? For example, Mark emphasizes the mystery and power of Jesus; in Matthew, he's the giver of the true Law; in Luke, he's the man for others; in John, he's the future cosmic Christ. This is where the fun of biblical study really starts.

The pretext What's *in front of* the text in terms of our own life situation as we encounter and digest this text? How might it speak to our own lives? What has it said to others and what does it say to us now?

If this sounds unduly complicated for a new reader of the Bible, it might serve to open up how many different questions we can ask of it. We don't expect people to jump through academic hoops whenever they encounter Scripture; it's enough to appreciate the possibilities of digging deeper into the Bible if they wish because, of course, we want to encourage people to love God with their *minds*.

3 Three levels

Many passages of Scripture are open to various levels of exploration and the ways in which we approach them will be determined by what we are doing with the passage (for example, preaching from it, leading a homegroup or suggesting it in a pastoral setting as devotional reading). The level we emphasize will also be affected by our own upbringing, our working theology and our personal preferences.

1 Face value In this approach, we simply trust what the text says and enjoy unpacking its significance for our own discipleship. The goal here is simply to grow in faith.

2 Theological meaning In this approach, we are seeking to understand the passage and its significance, both then and now, by asking some of those text, context, subtext and pretext questions above. The goal here is understanding.

3 Spiritual meaning In this approach, we look at the passage for its symbolic meaning, through its images and metaphors, and the ways in which it carries spiritual significance for us. It isn't so much the event the passage describes that matters, but what it suggests to the hungry heart. The goal here is spiritual nourishment.

A full sermon or Bible study might touch on all three of these levels of exploration, and the beauty of the divine conversation we have with Scripture is that it will affect each of us in a different way.

Quick idea: creating a visual map

A helpful way into a Bible story is to create a visual map of the Holy Land, by means of which members of a congregation can orientate themselves. In a traditional church, tell them they're looking down from the north – that is, looking towards Jerusalem from Galilee. (The Sea of Galilee itself may helpfully be by the font.) It's easy to point out the Mediterranean beyond the wall on one side of the church and the Jordan Valley coming down the opposite aisle. In the body of the church is the spine of Judaean hills leading to Samaria, with the mountains of Upper Galilee under the tower and beyond the west window. The pulpit is Jerusalem, with Bethlehem right behind and Jericho down to the right in the Jordan Valley. Qumran and the Dead Sea are further back again, with Egypt outside the east window (in the graveyard?) On the basis of this map, you can point out any of the main events of the Bible story, from the start of Abraham's journey from Ur of the Chaldees right through to the Ascension. It helps people to get a handle on where events took place and how they relate to one another. You can be sure of lightbulb moments occurring throughout the congregation.

How to read the Bible

Christian ministers, lay and ordained, will want to guide people to take the Bible seriously. But how? Some churches are very focused so that congregations are expected to use the Bible during the sermon, in both private prayer and homegroups, and perhaps in one-to-one mentoring. Other churches are a little more hit and miss. But here are various ways in which people may find themselves enriched by getting closer to the Bible and its messages.

Just reading
There's great value in simply exposing ourselves to Scripture and grasping something of the bigger story. Many people, from the Ethiopian eunuch on his way to Gaza (Acts 8.26–40), through great figures such as St Augustine, to modern-day readers who have been blown away by the Spirit as they've read part of the Bible, have discovered that unvarnished reading of this powerful book has changed their lives for ever. It might be good to suggest that readers start with Mark or Luke, go through Acts, then move on to Paul's Letter to the Philippians. A sequence like that gives readers a good grounding before they (hopefully) move on to Bible-reading notes. We can leave the rest up to the Holy Spirit.

Regular reading with notes
The discipline of reading the Bible daily, using notes from various sources, has languished somewhat in mainstream churches in recent years. There is, however, nothing as nourishing as being steeped in Scripture so that its words, images and truths become part of our very being, shaping our thinking and living. Some vigorous encouragement might be needed for a congregation for whom daily reading of the Bible is a minority pursuit – perhaps make a heavy pitch on Bible Sunday. Some examples are found below (see 'Resources').

Lectio divina (holy reading)
The Benedictine way of feeding on the Bible has come very much to the fore in recent years, and across the traditions. The purpose of such meditative reading of Scripture is not to gain *information* but to be open to *transformation*. It's the chewing

and digesting of a small section of Scripture that enables God to work within us to challenge, encourage and break us open to a deeper wisdom. There are four stages.

1 Read We take a passage and read it twice, noticing which word or phrase captures our attention.

2 Reflect We chew the phrase carefully, sucking all the goodness out of it. We look at it from different angles, ask difficult questions and shake it for its grace and truth.

3 Respond We then place before God any of the thoughts and feelings that have arisen while we've been thinking through the words of Scripture. It's the time to pray.

4 Rest If we want, we can simply then rest in the presence of God, encountered in his word.

Sensory meditation (Ignatian meditation)

This way of entering a gospel event through the imagination is richly appreciated by many, although it may not be possible for all. We use the senses to encounter Jesus in vivid and unpredictable ways. As ministers or leaders of groups, we may lead the meditation ourselves, but we'll also encourage people to do it on their own.

Read the passage, usually from one of the Gospels, in a slow and attentive manner This is done twice: once to remember the story, then again to begin entering it personally. Then close the Bible.

With closed eyes, we re-run the story from the standpoint of one of the disciples or of someone from the crowd. Using the 'baptized imagination', we watch the various people involved, their faces and reactions. We smell the sea air, listen to the voices, feel the rough stones underfoot. We let the story unfold slowly, noticing everything that happens and how people in the story respond.

Move closer to Jesus We can then get into a conversation with Jesus about what has just happened and let that conversation (prayer) carry on as long as is necessary. Then we disengage, return to the present and reflect on what we've learnt. And give thanks.

Tailpiece: the text of all texts

It is the text of all texts, the book which underlies almost all the great works of Western literature from the time of its compilation until the Enlightenment and beyond. Without a knowledge of it the great portion of Western architecture is incomprehensible. It is the key which unlocks the work of nearly all the painters, from Giotto to Blake. It is the libretto of Bach and Haydn and Beethoven. On battlefields, on deathbeds, in hospital wards and private households, rich and poor, its leaves have been turned, its pages opened, its well-known words have nourished and sustained countless human lives. In its poetry men and women have found echoes of their own heartbreak, their own doubt, their own dejection, their own sins, as well as a staff to comfort and a light to guide.[3]

B Bible

Resources

The resources are legion – and then some. The following are a just a few examples to work with, lend and commend.

John Barton, *What is the Bible?* (London: SPCK, 2009) and *A History of the Bible: The book and its faiths* (London: Allen Lane, 2019).

Bible Society, *The Bible Course* (available online at: <www.biblesociety.org.uk>).

John Bowker, *The Complete Bible Handbook* (London: Dorling Kindersley, 1998).

BRF, Bible-reading notes, published three times a year: *New Daylight*, *Guidelines* and *Day by Day with God* (Abingdon: BRF) (available online at: <www.biblereadingnotes.org.uk>).

John Goldingay, *The Old Testament for Everyone* (London: SPCK, 2016).

Reflections for Daily Prayer (London: Church House Publishing, published annually) (available online at: <www.chpublishing.co.uk/apps/reflections-for-daily-prayer>).

Vaughan Roberts, *God's Big Picture Bible: A Bible overview* (Downers Grove, IL: InterVarsity Press, 2009) (available online at: <www.clayton.tv/find/explore/1272/0i0/2924/>).

Scripture Union, *Daily Bread: Words for life* (Milton Keynes: Scripture Union, published quarterly) (available online at: <www.scriptureunion.org.uk>).

Simon Taylor, *How to Read the Bible (without switching off your brain)* (London: SPCK, 2015).

Tom Wright, *The New Testament for Everyone* (London: SPCK, 2019).

C

Care and compassion

David Nott is a surgeon who does extraordinary work in the midst of the most desperate theatres of war. In his book *War Doctor*, he tells of being invited to lunch at Buckingham Palace and sitting on the Queen's left. She turned to him and asked where he'd just come from. 'Aleppo,' he replied. She asked what it was like. 'My mind instantly filled with images of toxic dust, of crushed school desks, of bloodied and limbless children . . . My bottom lip started to go,' and he was unable to speak. The Queen touched his hand and then took some biscuits from a box in front of her. 'These are for the dogs,' she said. And for the rest of the lunch the Queen and the doctor fed and petted the corgis under the table. 'All the while we were stroking and petting them, and my anxiety and distress drained away. "There," the Queen said. "That's so much better than talking, isn't it?" '[1]

We could do no better than follow the sensitivity and compassion of the Queen as she responded to the grief welling up in her guest.

Pastoral care lies at the heart of everything we do in ministry. If we don't have a web of good relationships, characterized by mutual trust and concern, then our best intentions and thought-out plans may well come to grief. But more than that, care and compassion are the embodiment in ministry of the love of God to which we want passionately to bear witness.

The goal of good pastoral care is to help people thrive and grow in themselves, in their relationships and in their community. We do this through our own interactions and through the way our church life is structured for such care. But there are problems, such as the ones listed below.

- Pastoral care is sometimes seen as 'being nice' to people. That's candyfloss care, not the genuine article as demonstrated by Jesus.
- Pastoral care is sometimes only perceived as being given if the one offering it is an ordained priest or minister. This holds the ordained person to ransom and prevents the Church growing as the Body of Christ.
- In a fix-it culture, some people are only looking for 'answers' from experts, whereas pastoral care will often simply be about accompanying the person on their journey, and sometimes perhaps challenging their perceptions of it.
- We also have to recognize that we are moving ever deeper into a 'blame' culture, where every problem is somebody else's fault, and this can lead to complaints, grievance procedures, disciplinary measures, even litigation. In that context, offering pastoral care brings with it various new risks and can make people wary of getting involved.

Christians, however, are committed to the way of love, not as one option among others, but as the only option. 'As God's chosen ones, holy and beloved, clothe yourselves with compassion, kindness, humility, meekness and patience . . . Above all, clothe yourselves with love.' (Colossians 3.12–14). Love comes to be second nature to us because it's the first nature of God. It's the embodiment in the world of who God is.

The Roman Catholic theologian and palaeontologist Teilhard de Chardin wrote:

Some day, after mastering the winds, the waves, the tides and gravity, we shall harness for God the energies of love, and then, for the second time in the history of the world, man [sic] will have discovered fire.[2]

As ever, Christians are committed to anticipating that arrival and bringing that future into the present. We live to love.

It's been that way since the earliest days of the Church. The Emperor Julian (AD 332–363) persecuted Christians but he couldn't help noticing how the cause of Christianity:

has been specially advanced through the loving service rendered to strangers, and through their care for the burial of the dead. It is a scandal that there is not a single Jew who is a beggar, and that the godless Galileans care not only for their own poor but for ours as well, while those who belong to us look in vain for the help that we should render them.[3]

It's a long tradition.

It's obvious that wherever there are people, there will be needs, and those needs are infinite in number. We have to make them manageable in the context of our overall ministry. Only we can make the infinite finite. Alternatively, we may be the kind of person who doesn't really notice those needs, as Thomas Merton once recognized in himself: 'I trust God will put in my way ten million occasions for doing acts of charity, and if I'm smart, maybe I can catch seventeen of them in a lifetime before they get past my big, dumb face.'[4]. Sadly, I've met ministers who have been so caught up in their own agenda that they don't seem to notice other people's.

The needs are there. Look at any congregation on a Sunday morning (let alone the wider community) and you are actually looking at a huge number of issues, dilemmas, conflicts, anxiety, loneliness, depression, unresolved pain and much more. We shouldn't become overly stressed about this – humans are very resilient – but some people are crossing the burning sands and wild places of life, unaccompanied and bewildered, and those of us with faith will want to be there with them. In particular, we will want to be with them in a spirit of love and of hope – that distinctive Christian gift which never runs out.

Principles that guide our practice of pastoral care

Prayer

It's obvious that if we are seeking to embody love, then we must go to its source. Prayer undergirds our care and compassion and often enables Christians to go to remarkable lengths to demonstrate these qualities when others have long ago gone home. The ministry of Mother Teresa's home for the destitute and dying in Kolkata is an example. Visitors would go into the home where the temperature might be greater than forty degrees Celsius and the smell would be of disinfectant, curry and death, but they would see nuns and volunteers moving quietly and meditatively among the dying, tending to their needs. Visitors say there is an extraordinary sense of peace there. Grace fills the room. This kind of care can only emerge from the life of prayer that gives stability and strength to the nuns. In the same way, but in a less dramatic context, we too depend on the limitless love of God in the exercise of our ministry of pastoral care.

Presence

The people with whom we are wanting to identify in our pastoral care might not be aware of our prayer, but they will certainly be aware of whether or not we are fully present to them, giving them our fullest attention and not mentally wandering off to the next person or the next task (see **Attentiveness**). People have to know that we have time for them. Jack Nicholls, formerly Bishop of Sheffield, reported that, on his first day as a curate, his vicar said to him, 'I'd rather parishioners thought we were the two laziest priests in the Church of England than that they thought we didn't have time for them.' There's no substitute for this focused presence, and we can't fake it. Fundamentally, it's an attitude of heart. We must *be there*.

Listen

It's instructive to watch the risen Jesus encountering the two disciples on the road to Emmaus (Luke 24.13–35). He asks them what they were talking about and then what things have been happening in Jerusalem. He gives the disciples the dignity of telling their story and sharing their confusion with him and, in this way, Jesus could know what their needs actually were and how to respond. Jesus let them *tell him about himself*, and he still didn't interrupt.

Listening before talking is an essential principle of pastoral care. We may have a very good idea as to what would help someone, but until we hear it from the person concerned, it would be presumptuous to offer it. Watch Jesus again, this time with blind Bartimaeus outside Jericho (Luke 18.35–43). 'What do you want me to do for you?' asks Jesus. No presumption; he just gave Bartimaeus time to look at the implications of his desire for sight, since it would mean he would lose the status of a blind person dependent on gifts and would now have to work for a living. We can never know precisely how people we meet are perceiving their situation until we've heard them say it. Theologian Paul Tillich put it simply: 'The first duty of love is to listen.'

We may come to the realization that there's nothing we can actually do for someone except listen, but that listening may be all that's really needed from us. Pastoral care may simply consist of keeping sorrow company and it may be best to allow wounds to bleed for a while. In any case, 'advice' is usually the least helpful gift. Our solutions are not their solutions and only their solutions have a chance of helping. We might sensitively ask what they see as a range of possibilities in a given situation and work through them together, but the outcome must always be theirs. A useful phrase can be 'I wonder if . . .'. That gives others freedom to consider options without being given advice.

Alternatively, they might just want us to help them quietly play the blues.

Quick idea: setting up a pastoral visiting team

Caring for one another is the joyful responsibility of everyone in the Church, and although that care is often focused in the ministry of clergy and lay ministers, it can also be valuable to set up a pastoral visiting team to offer care to people in the congregation and beyond in the wider community. Members are likely to visit people who are elderly, housebound, bereaved, lonely or sick. The group should receive basic training in listening skills and some of the practicalities of setting up visits, follow-up and referrals. Supervision meetings are important, no matter how low-key, along with occasional gatherings for encouragement and further training. Everyone benefits.

Challenge

Responsible pastoral care doesn't always consist of supportive affirmation. If someone is on a path of self-destruction, it might be important to point that out. Appropriate challenge is an integral part of standing alongside someone if that person appears to be living in a self-deluded bubble. Our goal is to help people make decisions that will lead to them growing in self-confidence, honesty, authenticity and love. The key to this may well be helping them to discover a higher degree of self-awareness.

That self-awareness starts with the clergy and authorized ministers. I've been astonished at the priests I've sometimes met who have had a wholly unrealistic view of their own capabilities. A priest whose town congregation had steadily reduced from happy viability to single figures thought that he might apply to be principal of a theological college. There are others like him. Self-awareness starts at home, but then we offer whatever maturity we have attained to encourage others in their own growth.

Another challenge may take the form of putting clear boundaries around a pastoral relationship. Some situations have the potential to become unhealthy or dangerously exposed. When, where and how often we meet people will have to be considered, and sometimes each encounter needs to be recorded. We might have to insist that there's no playing games and draw attention to it when it crops up. Some people are adept at manipulation and might try to trap us into agreeing with them, affirming some action or responding to some declaration that they've made. One helpful guideline might be that we always have to speak the truth – but we don't always have to speak.

What all this amounts to is that Christian love isn't fluffy. It's love, all right, but there's a steel core to it.

Back-up

There is a particular danger in pastoral care: we're tempted to adopt a competence that we don't have, either because the other person puts us on a pedestal or because we have our own need to be needed. Unless we have proper training in counselling, with accreditation and supervision, there are situations where we will be out of our depth and must know how to refer people to proper professional help. There are, of course, trained resources for particular needs, such as Relate for relationship issues, Cruse for bereavement, and others. Most situations are within our competence and it's important not to denigrate the skills that we might have as trained pastors with the confidence and authorization of our denomination, but we must also know how to activate the back-up we'll sometimes need, not slip into believing we have the skill and experience for all the pastoral situations we face. There's also a welcome, if slow, recognition in many church organizations that regular supervision groups are a wise investment for everyone charged with pastoral ministry.

Endings
Christians in ministry are often poor at making good endings to particular pastoral relationships. It's understandable, because usually we go on seeing the person in our congregational life. But it may also be because we're too 'nice' to bring about a good ending to a more intense phase of care. The result can be dependence on the one side and an overloaded diary on the other. There are no hard-and-fast ways to bring about this ending; it simply requires clarity and determination.

Tailpiece: 'The power of love'
The following is the start of a sermon by Bishop Michael Curry at the wedding of Prince Harry and Meghan Markle, 2018.

The late Dr Martin Luther King Jr once said: 'We must discover the power of love, the redemptive power of love. And when we discover that, we will be able to make of this old world a new world, for love is the only way.'

There's power in love. Don't underestimate it. Don't even over-sentimentalize it. There's power – power in love. If you don't believe me, think about a time when you first fell in love. The whole world seemed to centre around you and your beloved. Oh there's power – power in love. Not just in its romantic forms, but any form, any shape of love. There's a certain sense that when you are loved, and you know it, when

---

someone cares for you, and you know it, when you love and you show it – it actually feels right. There's something right about it.

There is something right about it. And there's a reason for it. The reason has to do with the source. We were made by a power of love, and our lives were meant – and are meant – to be lived in that love. That's why we are here. Ultimately, the source of love is God himself, the source of all of our lives. There's an old medieval poem that says, 'Where true love is found, God himself is there.' The New Testament says it this way: 'Beloved, let us love one another, because love is of God, and those who love are born of God and know God. Those who do not love do not know God.' Why? 'For God is love.'

There's power in love. There's power in love to help and heal when nothing else can. There's power in love to lift up and liberate when nothing else will. There's power in love to show us the way to live.

Resources

Acorn Christian Healing Foundation, 'Just Listen!' course (available online at: <www.acornchristian.org>).

Justine Allain Chapman, *Resilient Pastors: The role of adversity in healing and growth* (London: SPCK, 2012).

Wesley Carr, *Handbook of Pastoral Studies* (London: SPCK, 1997).

Michael Jacobs, *Swift to Hear: Facilitating skills in listening and responding* (London: SPCK, 2000).

Paul Nash and Sally Nash, *Tools for Reflective Ministry* (London: SPCK, 2009).

Samuel Wells, *Incarnational Ministry* (London: Canterbury Press, 2017).

C

Children and schools

An evangelist was once asked how many people became Christians at a particular event. 'Two and a half,' he answered. 'You mean two adults and one child?' 'No,' said the evangelist, 'I mean two children and one adult. A child has a whole life to give to God. An adult's life is already half spent.'

Children are precious in the sight of God. Jesus said, 'Let the little children come to me and do not stop them; for it is to such as these that the kingdom of God belongs' (Luke 18.16).

Churches put enormous amounts of energy into ministry with children and there are many excellent resources to help (see 'Resources' below). What follows is just scraping the surface and can only try to identify issues and offer principles. Detail is available elsewhere. But it's undeniable that we've lost a lot of ground in recent decades, so first let's look honestly at some of the problems we face.

- Family life has become highly complex, with increased mobility and spending power. There's been an explosion in leisure options, including sport on Sunday mornings. Families go to see grandparents and take weekend breaks. In the increasing number of split families, children go to see their other parent. Regular church attendance has become more and more difficult, even if it were wanted.

- The British Social Attitudes survey told us in 2019 that 52 per cent of the population say that they have 'no religion'. The gulf between people of faith and those without faith has become awkwardly wide, and going to church has come to be a very unlikely choice for those without a background of belief. That isn't to say people claim to not have a spiritual side to their lives; they just don't associate it with conventional Christian belief and practice.
- Children and young families are surrounded by very smart technology at both home and school. The games industry is a multi-billion-pound bonanza for its techy entrepreneurs. We can summon up videos of people and places from anywhere in the world with a few clicks of a mouse or on our phone. In this sophisticated and expensive environment, most churches can't compete. Their worship and education facilities and practices seem to belong to another age.
- You need a critical mass of children or young families for others to feel welcome. When you drop below that figure, it takes great determination to be one of the few children who come. I write as one so determined to avoid going to Sunday school that my brother and I deliberately stung ourselves in a bed of nettles and returned home, pleading agony.

However, with a new social context come new opportunities.

Positives

- When the Christian story is little known, it comes with a freshness denied to those of us who have grown up with it and feel that we are on first-name terms with the Prodigal Son and even the fatted calf. God's story has real power.
- Children have a natural sense of the spiritual. Adults are often amazed at how responsive even young children can be when given a period of silence in a school assembly. Watch a small child be captivated by the colour and shape of a pile of stones on the beach, while the adults are running in and out

of the water and leaping on to surfboards. Not for nothing did Wordsworth write, 'Trailing clouds of glory do we come from God, who is our home.'[1] The trouble lies in what happens next. A child was overheard whispering to his baby brother, 'Tell me what God feels like. I'm starting to forget.' But when they're young, children have open hearts.

- Many schools are looking for help with religious education projects, and churches can offer both buildings and the time and skills of experienced older people. Schools are often looking for adults willing to get involved in reading with children or helping with musical productions. Fostering good relationships with schools is always worthwhile.
- In particular, church schools will usually be eager to form partnerships with local churches. Nearly a million children are in Anglican schools every day. This is an open door, and a gift horse not to be ignored.
- There are plenty of new approaches to working with children in a Christian context, ranging from Messy Church, Godly Play, Open the Book, Prayer Spaces in Schools, Experience Easter/Christmas, mentoring and more, through to the well-established parent and toddler groups, breakfast and after-school clubs and holiday weeks.

But what lies behind all this activity? What principles should guide our work with God's favoured ones? Here are some.

Guiding principles
In our ministry with children and young families, we need to 'run with the culture' rather than, Canute like, try to reverse it We have to go with the grain of society's Sunday mornings and adapt our offering. Midweek events and services at 4 p.m. on Sundays have been found to be attractive. Nor can we compete with sophisticated and expensive educational tools and technology, at least not to the same degree as at home and

school. We can concentrate on relationships, though, and that, ultimately, wins out over everything.

We need to offer an experience of church that's as good as we can make it, but also go to where the children are, physically and mentally. I've often encouraged school chaplains (increasingly found in state schools as well as independent schools) by telling them that they might be in touch with hundreds of children a week, while the parish priest or minister may have only a handful in a church group. How can we support chaplains? How can we get more chaplains in primary schools? Then there's sport – a major obsession for children. A church in Buckinghamshire has a Saturday morning football club with more than a hundred children in teams and playing in leagues. And if children are deeply attached to technology, we need to engage with it as much as possible because it fascinates children and young people. Our approach, then, should be to go with the culture, if it's not illegal, immoral or directly anti-Christian.

Trust a child's innate spirituality As above, use silence, symbols, songs and sacraments. Children get it! Candles cast a spell. A hazelnut is full of mystery; there's a world in the life cycle of a butterfly; Taizé music enchants; African drums excite; silence captivates – all to the glory of God. The careful child-friendly use of the sacrament of Holy Communion can bring children into the mystery that could sustain them for a lifetime.

Focus on Jesus It's the Christ in Christianity that matters. But not the Jesus portrayed by old pictures on tired walls in many a church building. This extraordinary figure needs to step out of the past and into the children's present, off the pages and into their lives. Hopefully, they will be more interested in him, his story and his present reality than in the fact that it's the twelfth Sunday after Trinity.

Recognize that church life may have to be made up of events rather than long-running programmes Weekends are so packed with various activities that 'regularity' at church encompasses not only a child who's there every week but also one who's there twice a month or sometimes only once a month. It may be better, therefore, to think of one-off events that have real impact than ongoing programmes. A holiday week or an event on Good Friday may be a more effective use of resources than such programmes. One church has a two-monthly event called Bounce with a wide range of fun, physical activities to which children can invite their friends. Others pick up on major sporting occasions and have family fun days with large television screens. Relationships are made, with openings for further contact.

> **Quick idea: setting up a school/church liaison group**
>
> If the school is a church school (and a quarter of primary schools 'belong' to the Church of England) or if there is a friendly welcome from any school, church-affiliated or not, see if a school/church liaison group could be set up to explore different ways in which they could enrich each other's work. Plans could include: holiday clubs or fun days, mentoring, Open the Book, reading assistants, midweek use of the church as a teaching aid for Christmas or Easter, musical or artistic participation in worship on special Sundays, community service of various kinds and much more. Of course, such a liaison group would depend completely on relationships of trust and respect.

Build on special days that crop up throughout the year If we're living in this 'event' culture, we might identify various special days on which we could enrich our worship so that it incorporates the needs of children more intentionally. Going through the year, we have the baptism of Jesus, the start of Lent, Mothers' Day (if we're not too purist), Good Friday, Easter,

Pentecost, Fathers' Day, Harvest, Remembrance, Advent and Christmas. That makes eleven possibilities, to which we can add one of our own, such as the dedication festival of our church. Imaginative worship teams could make something special and memorable of some of these occasions, and make children feel that church is a good place to be. Local schools can always be invited to participate in music, drama and so on.

Be relational Talk to many Christian adults and you'll find that they had a particular person or group they related to as children and this had a lasting effect on them and their growth in faith. It's people, not schemes, plans and strategies that change lives. Leaders who inspire affection are the alchemists of faith. Who do you remember?

Be professional As far as possible. This will mean having proper safeguarding policies in place, together with health and safety measures, quality materials and clear outlines for a session, event or outing. This should, by now, be the bedrock of any church-related activity. So, do we have proper policies and designated responsibilities?

Know what's out there There's a huge range of supportive resources available to us as we engage in children's ministry (see 'Resources' below). Our task is not to reinvent the wheel in children's work or to get into our own furrow and keep ploughing it indefinitely. There are training courses, workshops and networks for the team. There are books, online resources, magazines, videos and ideas to last a lifetime. But someone on the team needs to know about them.

Concentrate on experience more than content In the last resort, an encounter with God is more important than learning more about what Christians believe. Information can come later;

what's needed first is an encounter with God and God's community. Yet, a lot of our approach to children's work is geared towards teaching rather than encountering. There's no substitute for spiritual experience appropriate to the age and stage of a child's life and the embrace of a loving community. The experience of being loved by God and God's community is more transformational than anything else. A man told his vicar that his son had forsaken God. 'What shall we do?' he asked. 'Love him more than ever,' came the reply.

If possible, fund a children and families worker For a small church this is obviously out of the question, although groups of churches often manage to make an appointment together. A considerable number of trained children's workers are emerging from courses across the country every year. Research shows, not surprisingly, that having lively children's work is a major factor in a church growing in numbers. Funding a worker is a tangible investment in the future.

Tailpiece: the spiritual wisdom of children

Anna, a child whose age was still in single figures, told her friend Fynn about her understanding of 'Mister God.' [Hopefully it was a responsible, safeguarded relationship.]

'Fynn, Mister God doesn't love us.' She hesitated. 'He doesn't really, you know, only people can love. I love Bossy [the cat], but Bossy don't love me. I love you, Fynn, and you love me, don't you? You love me because you are people. I love Mister God truly, but he don't love me.'

It sounded like a death knell. Why does this have to happen to people? Now she's lost everything. But I was wrong. She had got both feet planted firmly on the next stepping stone.

'No,' she went on, 'no, he don't love me, not like you do, it's different, it's millions of times bigger. Fynn, you can love better than any people that ever was, and so can I, can't I? But Mister God is different. You see, Fynn, people can only love outside and can only kiss outside, but Mister God can love you right inside, and Mister God can kiss you right inside, so it's different. Mister God ain't like us; we are a little bit like Mister God, but not much yet.'[2]

Jesus said, 'Unless you change and become like children, you will never enter the kingdom of heaven' (Matthew 18.3).

Resources

BRF, Messy Church (<www.brf.org.uk/messy-church>). Masses of excellent information.

Godly Play (<www.godlyplay.uk>). Rich, sensory encounter with God through Bible stories.

Grove Books (<www.grovebooks.co.uk/collections/education>). A wide range of valuable titles.

Rebecca Nye, *Children's Spirituality: What it is and why it matters* (London: Church House Publishing, 2009).

YCW, *Youth and Children's Work*, magazine (plus downloads available online at: <www.youthandchildrens.work>).

Every Anglican diocese has someone with children and families responsibility, and similar arrangements will operate in other churches. See diocese or church websites.

D

Death and bereavement

A register of deaths in Lamplugh Parish in the Lake District between 1658 and 1663 gave these statistics: Frightened to death by fairies – 3 deaths, Bewitched – 4 deaths, Old women drowned after trial for witchcraft – 3 deaths, Led into a horse pond by a will o' the wisp – 1 death.

If these seem unlikely causes, the reality of death isn't at all unlikely. As Julian Barnes puts it: 'Death never lets you down, remains on call seven days a week, and is happy to work three consecutive eight-hour shifts. You would buy shares in death if they were available; you would bet on it.'[1]

In what follows, I'll conflate the Church's ministry with the dying and its ministry with the bereaved. That is because the issues often overlap, but look out for sections that are situation-specific.

How we deal with death
Denial and delay
We deny it by keeping it out of our conversation or using coded language. We package it up and hand it over to professionals. We try to delay it by following every change in dietary and medical advice that comes along. But still it remains the dark wind from

our future (Camus) or the background music playing faintly but constantly in the distance (Heidegger).

Stoicism

For people without faith there's a noble tradition of stoicism about death. The atheist philosopher Bertrand Russell wrote about his death: 'There is darkness without and when I die there will be darkness within. There is no splendour, no vastness anywhere, only triviality for a moment and then nothing.'[2] This stoicism is a hard road to follow, but in the absence of faith, it's realistic and courageous.

Humour

When we're younger, we sometimes find humour puts death in its place. Do you know the one about the funeral director who signed his letters, 'Yours eventually'? Or the doggerel:

Each time I'm near a church
I walk in for a visit
So that when at last I'm carried in
The Lord won't say 'Who is it?'[3]

When we're older, this strategy of humour doesn't work so well.

Faith

Christians are able to face death with hope. Of course, we might well, and reasonably, be fearful of the process of dying, but belief in the resurrection of Christ and our resurrection in him, changes the whole dynamic of death. Dietrich Bonhoeffer called death 'the supreme festival on the road to freedom.'[4] Among the last words of the well-known American pastor Eugene Peterson were, 'Let's go!' Moreover, facing death with faith can give more colour and texture to life. The psychologist Carl Jung was known to say that we can't live properly until we know how to die, a conviction shared by Denise Inge in her own terminal illness when she wrote, 'Death is a crucial part of the human condition: when we avoid talking about death we avoid talking about life.'[5]

All these ways of facing death will be in the background of our thinking as we get involved in ministry with the dying and bereaved.

Quick idea: death cafés

There has been a marked interest in recent years in death cafés or other opportunities to discuss death in an open, healthy and constructive way. Such an event could fit into café church, a homegroup, a lunch club or be a special one-off. There's plenty of good material on the Internet (just enter 'death café'), but the Church of England has produced an excellent resource in its Grave Talk material, which includes a facilitator's guide and a set of excellent discussion cards to use at such an event (see 'Resources' below). These discussions consistently turn out to be valuable, enjoyable, and full of laughter. They are also remarkably life-affirming.

Four types of interaction

In an unavoidable simplification of this complex ministry, there are likely to be different types of interaction with the dying and bereaved. We have to judge which is appropriate, and when.

1 Practical

There are many practical tasks in which a church and its representatives can offer unfussy help. Providing meals, phoning people, cancelling commitments, answering the phone and the door, and so on. The key is in that word 'unfussy'. A quiet usefulness is what's needed, and church members are among those well placed to offer it.

2 Emotional

We will be aware of the grief cycle that runs, with variations, through the stages of shock/denial – anger – bargaining/if only – depression – acceptance – adapted life, but telling people where they are on the cycle isn't likely to win you many friends. The key word rather is 'presence'. Emotions may be raw and complicated, so being with people in terminal illness or with those recently bereaved requires sharply attuned emotional antennae.

What is required emotionally at this time? With someone who's dying it may well be that he or she will want the opportunity to say some of the following:

- thank you
- I'm sorry
- I forgive you
- I love you.

We might be able to facilitate those tender conversations. Emotional intelligence will also enable us to know when to speak and when to be silent. Hopefully, we know not to contradict the bereaved person, even if they say things that we disagree with. We have to start with people's 'ordinary theology' and maybe work it round to a more constructive place.

A bereaved person may want to talk or may just want silent companionship. There may be need for reassurance about numbness, anger, guilt or other emotions. We might make the following suggestions to the bereaved.

- A flood of different emotions is normal. Let them be and they'll find their own level eventually.
- Some days the emotional fallout will seem like quantities of rubbish strewn all over a beach, and the next day the tide might have swept the beach clean. You never know how these emotions will come and go from day to day, but that's OK – even if the waves sometimes knock you over.
- Be gentle with yourself. Your path through all this is uniquely

your own, so you do it your own way. People might advise all sorts of things but there are no blueprints for bereavement, so don't be afraid of being your own guide.

- Try to reconnect with the person as he or she was before the terminal illness. What was the 'essence' of that person? What sort of epitaph would that person have wanted? What were the best times?

Good pastoral care by a church will then probably gather around such things as follow-up visiting, an invitation to a bereavement support group if that seems appropriate, and an annual service of memory and hope, usually around All Saints Day at the beginning of November. Of course, this time can also offer a bereaved person the opportunity to reconsider faith and perhaps come to church, where a sensitive welcome can be offered and friendships may be made.

3 Spiritual

The funeral is of course the time when we are able to focus the spiritual resources of the Church on the complexities that surround a death. The service will have elements of thanksgiving and celebration, community and family memory, pastoral care and release, all in the context of Christian hope and the embracing love of God. There are excellent books on religious funerals (see 'Resources' below) but the changes taking place in society's funeral practice more widely have to be acknowledged and given considered response. It isn't sufficient to lament the loss of the Church's near monopoly on funerals. The movement towards non-religious funerals should be a challenge to us to recognize the desire for more flexibility and humanity in the style of Christian funerals, but we shouldn't lose confidence in the abiding emotional and spiritual strength of what we have to offer. Many people want prayer, faith and dignity to be part of the event, but don't want it in a stuffy, overloaded religious package.

The great resources we have here are the cross and resurrection, together with prayer and sacrament, but we have to offer these with great sensitivity to what dying or bereaved people need and want. A wodge of doctrine is unlikely to serve them or the gospel very well. Nevertheless, the living reality of these resources are capable of transforming people's experience of death and bereavement. And if we deploy them well, those with whom we share them will take hold of them with seriousness, because they are some of the only hopeful offerings in these times of darkness.

Cross God knows; he's been there. God is here; he loves you. These are the simple, profound, healing truths at the heart of the cross. We offer them with humility and care but with confidence for they carry their own conviction. Words of Archbishop William Temple still ring true:

> There can't be a God of love, men [*sic*] say, because if there was and he looked upon the world, his heart would break. The Church points to the cross and says, 'It did break.' It's God who made the world, men say. It's he who should bear the load. The Church points to the cross and says, 'He did bear it.'

The cross is the eternal sign that God suffers with us. We are not alone in our anguish. It will often be appreciated if we leave a small hand-cross with someone who's dying .

Resurrection It's the firm Christian conviction that death is not the end. The resurrection is the USP (unique selling point) of Christianity, yet we are often very cautious about sharing that confidence. In part, that demonstrates pastoral sensitivity; we don't want to load our theology on to vulnerable people. But there are ways of being both sensitive *and* confident. In any case, our role is not just to be pastoral counsellors; we are Christians who have a message of hope for the world that rests in the dying and rising of the Son of Man. The New Testament emerged from a bereaved community that had discovered a whole new understanding of death through the resurrection of Jesus. The disciples were gripped with an overwhelming belief that death had been defeated, and we bear witness to that conviction at this crucial moment of transition in people's lives.

The issue that then becomes important is the way that we should speak about these things. The key is to engage with people's actual questions and their 'intuitive theologies' rather than to tell them what they should believe. If we take what they think seriously, and work with it, we are likely to be more helpful than if we have a set of right answers. The question to ask is, 'What's getting people through this dark time?' Then we can look for God together in their answers. For example, many people say they believe in some form of reincarnation; others believe that death leads to a long sleep or rest, with the idea of eternal docility lying behind it. So let's work with those as the starting points. Again, the idea of angels is never far away in popular ideas about death and beyond. A third of British people believe they have a guardian angel and one in ten claims to have met an angel. In the USA, the figures are much higher again. So let's work with that. After all, there's a strong Christian tradition of the communion of saints, the heavenly host, the cloud of witnesses.

Ultimately, we will hope in our conversations to arrive at the resurrection of Jesus and the convictions of 1 Corinthians 15. If Jesus has been raised from the dead, so it will be for us. What form that will take is not clear of course, but Paul gives us the image of the grain of wheat that dies in the ground and then appears in a quite different form. Our future therefore lies in being a 'spiritual body' – that is, not the body as we know it, but not a free-floating 'soul' or disembodied spirit either – a Greek, not a Hebrew concept. The Judaeo/Christian idea is of *being* a soul rather than *having* one. Remember, the only image

Jesus uses consistently is of a banquet. (The Revd Sydney Smith expanded this to 'eating pâté de fois gras to the sound of trumpets,' but that may not be an image to offer.)

The way that we talk about these ideas needs to engage with the intuitions of those we're with and how they're thinking. We mustn't talk over or talk down. As we explore these things, we can then carefully introduce Christian ideas, the keynote of which will be hope. We really don't know what life in God will be like, except that when we experience it, we'll probably say 'Of course!'

Prayer and sacrament These are basic resources we have to offer someone who's near death. Again, we have to offer them sensitively, without assuming that the world-view of those we're with is the same as ours. A combination of a psalm, a well-tried traditional prayer, an extempore prayer suitable to the situation, and a blessing, is often all that's needed. Anointing can be deeply reassuring or the confirmation of a death sentence, so it must be offered carefully. For devout Christians, it's possible that nothing will matter more than a very simple Communion.

4 Intellectual

It's unlikely that a person in a terminal stage of life is going to want to get into an intellectual discussion about the nature and causes of suffering. At a later stage, however, some bereaved people may want to visit the perceived unfairness or cruelty of their recent experience. It's then that a discussion of God's action in the world, the nature and cost of freedom, and the purpose and effectiveness of prayer, might occur. This hugely important issue is discussed in **Suffering.**

Tailpiece: a true story

Jon was a hospice chaplain and had visited Samuel for six months when, sadly, he died. Jon took the graveside service and afterwards he stood silently with Samuel's devastated son Henri. As they stood there, a yellow swallowtail butterfly fluttered overhead and landed on the casket. Jon turned to the boy and said, 'Look, I said you'd have a sign that your dad would be OK, and there's a sign.' Henri looked at Jon with contempt and said, 'A bug lands on my dad's casket and that's supposed to mean something to me? You're pathetic.' The boy turned and walked away. Jon drove home overwhelmed with despair, feeling like a failure as a chaplain. He prayed for Henri.

When Jon got home, his mobile phone went off. It was Henri's mother, Marion. 'I need you to come over to our house right now,' she said. Sensing the urgency, Jon went. When he got there, the door was open and he went straight in. Marion called from the room in which Samuel had died. Jon carefully opened the door and stared in amazement. The room was filled with butterflies, yellow, broad-winged swallowtail butterflies, on the bed, the side table, Marion's shoulders, in and out of the window, everywhere.

Henri was sitting in a rocking chair by his father's bed, rocking back and forth, laughing and crying, laughing and crying.[6]

Resources

Jeremy Brooks, *Heaven's Morning Breaks: Sensitive and practical reflections on funeral practice* (Stowmarket: Kevin Mayhew, 2013).

Joanna Collicutt, Lucy Moore, Martyn Payne and Victoria Slater, *Seriously Messy: Making space for families to talk together about life and death* (Abingdon: BRF, 2019).

Cruse Bereavement Care (<www.cruse.org.uk>). Counselling for people working through grief.

The Church of England, 'Funerals' (<www.gravetalk.org>). A simple way to help people to talk about death, dying and funerals.

DeathLife (<www.deathlife.org.uk>). Multiple resources on death and dying for ministry, including a course, Bible studies, sermon starters, a prayer walk, art, poetry, recorded meditations and the course handbook *Well Prepared*.

Mark Oakley, *Readings for Funerals* (London: SPCK, 2015).

Stephen Oliver (ed.), *Inside Grief* (London: SPCK, 2013).

E

Evangelism

We struggle with this. We do church; we do pastoral care; we do social concern. But we're not sure how to do evangelism that isn't either manipulative or embarrassing. Some find that, although they started out as fishers of men and women, for various reasons they've ended up as shepherds instead.

And it's risky work. We probably sympathize with the priest who started his sermon, 'Our subject today is how to win the world for Christ with the minimum of fuss and bother.'

If we think back to our own experience of coming to a living faith, most of us would be able to identify some intentional change in direction, some event, series of events or process by which we came to a new relationship with God. In evangelism, we're trying to help others to find their way to that change.

What is evangelism?
Evangelism is the process by which people become disciples of Jesus Christ. It's a subset of mission but not the same thing (see **Mission**). Evangelism is inviting people to come under the just and gentle rule of God in every part of their lives. Justin Welby, as Archbishop of Canterbury, said, 'The best decision that any human being can ever make in their life anywhere in the world,

in any circumstances, whoever they are, is to follow Jesus Christ as their Lord.'[1]

One way to see the various moves a person might make towards being a follower of Jesus is as follows.

Once-born Christians These are people who have always believed and gone to church, gently growing in their faith and their practice of it.

Twice-born Christians These are 'born-again' Christians who have had a radical, life-changing experience of coming to faith, something that might act as an anchor throughout their lives.

'Once-and-a-half' born Christians These are people like me who had an attachment to the Church but who, at a particular stage, took on the gift and opportunity of personal faith for themselves. We were always in touch with faith but only later made it our own.

We need to find words and images that are appropriate to different people and different situations. The New Testament uses many images for what happens when someone becomes a Christian. It's 'knowing Christ' (Philippians 3.10), 'receiving Christ' (Revelation 3.20), 'coming to Christ' (John 6.37), being 'in Christ' (2 Corinthians 5.17), Christ being 'in us' (Galatians 2.20), 'putting on' Christ (Romans 13.14) or simply 'following' Christ (Matthew 4.19). The important thing is to be in a close relationship with Christ in a way that changes all that we are and do. Evangelism is helping people to enter or discover that relationship.

Motivation for evangelism

Many motivations aren't worthy of this noble task, such as to want to be a so-called successful church or to replace those in the congregation who've died or to help balance the church's finances. These are not motivations that will look good on the day of judgement.

Better would be the desire to share something that's been truly life changing. It's not hard to let friends know about a great film, a new book or a wonderful holiday destination. It happens naturally. So it is with being a Christian.

Best of all as a motivation is love. Evangelism that takes place as the overflow of a heart that's full of the love of God makes evangelism as natural as the sun rising on a new day. Letting people know that God loves them without hesitation is a delight and a privilege. This can happen in a whole congregation too; if there's a rise in the spiritual temperature of a church and it gets really hot, then evangelism and renewal just happen naturally. Evangelism has to be seen as coming out of relationships and friendships. 'Trying to convert' someone is wrestling, not dancing; it's selling something rather than inviting someone into a friendship.

One thing we must always remember, however, is that numbers on their own can never be the success criterion of a faith centred on a man who was crucified. At the heart of the Christian faith is a cross, a sign of pain, humiliation and failure. We do well to remember the words of Bonhoeffer that 'when Jesus calls a man [sic] to follow him, he bids him come and die'.[2] The invitation we make in evangelism isn't to a trouble-free fun run through life, but to the serious and infinitely rewarding experience of following Jesus, both crucified and risen. We would love more people to share that experience with us, but not in an uninformed way that doesn't reckon with the cost of doing so.

Quick idea: praying for others

Invite members of the congregation to pray regularly for two or three particular people they know who don't share their faith. Give them cards on which to write those names and place in a spot where prayer is natural, be it in the kitchen or a chair in the living room or just a coat pocket for when they go out. Feed in regular reminders and encouragements, including different ways to pray for those people. Some people might want to meet as a pair or a triplet for shared prayer. After several weeks, or even a few months, give people an opportunity to report back, without naming names, about what has happened. Have there been conversations about faith? Has there been attendance at some Christian event? An opportunity to lend a book? A decision to come to church? Keep praying. People come to faith mainly through friendships.

How do we do it?

We used to speak about a process like that described below.

Believing – belonging – behaving

You first came to intellectual belief, which would bring you to belong to a church, which would then lead to a Christian way of life. Sometimes it seemed as if 'behave' came first! We then found that a more likely process was the following.

Blessing – belonging – believing – behaving

If we bless people with genuine care, this may lead to belonging to a church, in which context faith might be discovered and so lives could be shaped around Jesus and his teaching.

In today's culture of suspicion around religion and other truth claims, we probably need to think in terms of a more realistic process like the cycle diagram shown here.

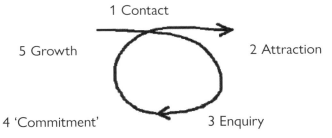

1 Contact

5 Growth

2 Attraction

4 'Commitment'

3 Enquiry

Contact

Every church community has a large number of existing relationships either corporately (groups that use the church premises) or individually (people we know). Between us we might be in contact with reading groups, art classes, civic societies, choirs, parents and toddler groups, school parents, gym users, walking groups, U3A, non-churchgoing partners and so on. Once we work it out, we have heaps of contacts.

Attraction

The question then is, 'How can we be such an interesting church community that people want to find out more about what makes us tick?' It could be through the reputation we have as a place of genuine commitment to the well-being of the community or our engagement with major issues, such as food poverty, climate change, homelessness. Alternatively, it could be that we have interesting programmes and events. Perhaps we have a reputation for sensitive and imaginative worship. We handled a baptism or funeral well. We're committed to work with children or the elderly and with people suffering with dementia or carers. Maybe we're open-minded, encourage questions and avoid easy answers or, simply, we're friendly. Whatever it is, we can hope to be an attractive community, what you might call a 'community of grace', where people might catch the scent of some long-forgotten hope.

Enquiry

We then hope that people will be sufficiently interested to be open to some level of 'uncommitted involvement'. The Holy Spirit is always at work so some people will be ready for an enquirer's course, such as Alpha or Pilgrim. It has to be publicized, and personal invitations are given to those with whom the church has had some tangential contact. It might also be good to offer the course as a refresher for people already in the congregation; a reminder of the basics rarely goes amiss. Every church probably ought to have such a course available at least once a year.

One church organized a 'Questions Children Ask' event aimed at school parents (we don't have to know all the answers); another church organized a 'Big Questions' session in a coffee shop; another church set up an event in a working men's club with the title, 'Is there hope in a world under pressure?'; you can 'grill a bishop' in a local pub; while a community barbecue can strengthen relationships. How about a quiz evening, *Desert Island Discs* or a talent evening? Small dinner parties give an opportunity for discussion after a short testimony. Another church had a group called 'No Holds Barred' for anyone interested in faith questions or anyone hanging on to faith by their fingernails. This group was self-run, with no right or wrong answers, and accompanied by good coffee, high-quality biscuits and the occasional whiskey.

Language A word about the language we use at this stage of exploration. It's very important that when we get near to spiritual issues, we don't resort to the coded language we use between ourselves. Words such as sin, salvation, repentance, righteousness or judgement usually need to be avoided on pain of a large fine. We need normal language, to decode and decipher the language of Zion, and to find words and images that chime in with people's ordinary experiences and instincts. After all, as Brian McLaren writes,

> Paul never shared 'the Four Spiritual Laws.' John never invited anyone to come forward and say a sinner's prayer so they could be born again. Peter never explained the four or five simple 'steps to peace with God.' St Augustine never invited anyone to pray with him to receive Christ as personal saviour. Martin Luther never issued an altar

call. Jesus himself never told anyone 'how to become a Christian.'[3]

We must choose our language with care.

Style is just as important The exploration of faith shouldn't be a sales pitch, monologue, entertainment, guilt trip or bullet-proof argument. It should be conversation, friendship, opportunity, question, invitation or story. That's how people enquire these days and the liquid gold of the gospel has then to be put into the new moulds of today's culture.

Commitment

This is a sensitive stage and particularly open to clumsy embarrassment. Moreover, people might be interested in discussing faith without wanting to take it further and make it personal. It would be wonderful if we could know that sharing our confidence in God's unconditional love would be enough. Sometimes it is. After all, we understand enough about psychology to realize that knowing ourselves to be loved is often transformative.

However, missing this commitment stage of the cycle could also be the spiritual equivalent of leaving a bride at the altar. Moving the analogy on a bit, in childbirth the midwife spends most of her time around the edges of the action, letting nature do what it does, but there comes a moment when the midwife has to say 'push'. What might we do to help people take this step? Baptism is an obvious moment for adults and, if that has already taken place, confirmation is another gift for Anglicans. These events have to be seen not as simple rites of passage without significant implications. These are moments to cross the line.

There are less formal settings too. If we're running an enquirers' course, there may be a residential element or a retreat day and this is when the possibility of making a response to what has been discovered on the course can be offered. According to taste, we can offer one-to-one prayer, a prayer to echo in the heart, a symbolic action (taking a small cross, lighting a candle), receiving a book and so on.

It's vital that there is no manipulation and people realize this is only one (significant) step on a journey they have been on already and that will continue for ever. Indeed, in a sense we have to turn to Christ every day, to stand with him again and see the world with his eyes. So it's wise not to push too hard at this point of commitment. The Holy Spirit is in charge and needs to be trusted. When people are ready to move on, we should be ready to help them – but not before.

It's also important to emphasize that commitment isn't a matter of believing everything at once or believing six impossible things before breakfast. Faith is about a way of life more than a block of beliefs. It's about following Jesus and 'being covered in the dust of our rabbi' more than signing on the dotted line of doctrine. Questions continue. The journey goes on.

Growth

People who have become Christians or taken some significant step in their spiritual journey mustn't just be left there. As with all living things, if we don't grow, we die. There are many discipleship courses around, including some of those mentioned above. Several dioceses and denominations have their own. Often the best kind of course for growth, however, comes from the local context, where local factors guide the choice of material and it feels more authentic than a distant 'off-the-peg' model. A weekly, fortnightly or monthly ongoing course is hugely valuable. Many churches encourage continuing growth through homegroups, prayer groups, training mornings, retreats, weekends and festival weeks.

But congregations beware – new Christians might ask awkward questions of existing practices. Those questions will be important, and most definitely mustn't be treated as 'the naive questions of those who will soon learn our ways'. If the church is alive, it will be open to change as much as those new Christians are hopefully open to growth.

Tailpiece: Aiden the missionary

Aidan, the saintly founder of the community on Lindisfarne in AD 635, wandered the countryside on missionary journeys. As he met people he would ask, 'Do you love God?' If they said yes, he would say, 'Then love him more.' If they said no, he would say, 'Then can I tell you about Jesus?'

Resources

Alpha course (<www.alpha.org>).

Church House Publishing, *Emmaus: The way of faith* course (London: CHP, 2010) (available online at: <www.chpublishing.co.uk>).

Stephen Cottrell, *From the Abundance of the Heart: Catholic evangelism for all Christians* (London: Darton, Longman & Todd, 2006).

Vincent Donovan, *Christianity Rediscovered* (London: SCM Press, 2001). A classic on mission strategy.

Mark Ireland and Mike Booker, *Making New Disciples: Exploring the paradoxes of evangelism* (London: SPCK, 2015).

Pilgrim course (<www.pilgrimcourse.org>).

Thy Kingdom Come, 'Evangelism for the Local Church', prayer resource (available online at: <www.thykingdomcome.global/resources/evangelism-local-church>)

F

Forgiveness

On the shore of the Sea of Galilee is the church of St Peter's Primacy, so called because it's where, by tradition, Jesus forgave Peter and reinstated him to his key role in the future of the Jesus movement. In the afternoon, when the pilgrimage buses have gone, it's a beautiful, quiet spot with a view down the whole length of the lake. It's also an evocative place for reflecting on the important ministry of forgiveness, demonstrated so sensitively here by Jesus. We'll look at that in a moment.

Many people need to know that they themselves are forgiven, and others need to find a way to forgive. These issues may only emerge in deep pastoral encounters and we have to be alert to those tender spots where these issues might be lurking. We then have a range of strategies available, ranging from prayer and formal confession to professional counselling and therapy. The one thing we must be clear about is that we might be dislodging some volatile and explosive material.

We'll take the issue of forgiveness from the two perspectives of *receiving* forgiveness and *declaring* forgiveness.

Receiving forgiveness

Of course, we live in a culture in strong denial about our need for forgiveness. People prefer to believe that we do messy things or we've just been made this way or we were brought up badly or we were led astray or we were mistreated and so on. It's anything but our fault. The result is that we've exchanged the forgiveness of sins for the blaming of others.

Rather more honesty is required. While it's important that the local church doesn't 'bang on' about sin, and in most situations needs to find other words to describe it, it's nevertheless vital that we don't succumb to the siren voices that tell us all is well. It isn't. We are flawed people living in a broken world and we need a saviour – not an adviser or a life-coach but a saviour.

The DJ called Moby, who has sold more than 20 million albums, once said, 'I thought the teachings of Christ were basically "Everything's OK, don't worry, you're doing great – just try to be nice to squirrels occasionally."' But then he read the New Testament and got a more comprehensive understanding of human nature.[1] All is not as well as we'd like to think.

Forgiveness is the heart of the gospel. It's the great liberator, the gateway to life in abundance. But first we have to reckon with the problem that forgiveness deals with. Here are some tests of how we're doing in the grey areas of our lives.

- How would we feel if our family and best friends were able to sit down and watch a video of not only all that we've done in the last week, but all that we'd thought as well? How comfortable would we feel?
- Try the plumb line of truth. How true have we been this week to ourselves, the true selves God made us to be, the authentic 'me'? How true have we been to others in our dealings with them? Has the compass always pointed to true north? How true have we been to the wider needs of society, crying out for active engagement over poverty, climate change, asylum seekers, domestic abuse and so on. If the plumb line of personal truth is about love and authenticity, how true have we been?

- If one understanding of sin is that it's the absence of love, how have we been in our loving over this last week – loving our neighbour (that's good), loving those in need (that's our calling), loving those better off than ourselves (that's saintly) and loving our enemies (that's God's love and it conquers the world). Love is a good measure.
- The Jesuit Examen asks us to look not just at the times when we've felt positive, connected, grateful and alive but also at the times when we've felt disconnected, low, diminished, depressed and frustrated. What was going on there? Was it something we got wrong? What was God saying to us?

Nevertheless, if forgiveness is the heart of the gospel, God's love is the 'heart of the heart' of the gospel. This is where Jesus' post-resurrection, post-breakfast conversation with Peter is so refreshing. What Jesus wanted wasn't the opportunity to tell Peter off and make him grovel. He wanted to restore a relationship. So he went back to the beginning. 'Simon, son of John' – his original name – 'do you love me?' (John 21.16). It's love that restores relationship, so Jesus simply asked that warm, generous question.

God doesn't keep a tally of our misdemeanours to wave in front of us on the day of judgement. Neither should the Church be in the business of sin management, digging out sins that it can then forgive, satisfying its own self-righteousness. Our ministry is about helping people into wholeness, and the Christian's medicine of choice is love, because nothing is more transformative than love, as Peter experienced on that beach.

When we offer *baptism*, therefore, we're using wonderfully rich imagery. The candidate goes down into the waters where the old self, the one that does as it likes and thinks it's the centre of the universe (the Big Me), dies. The person goes under the water, 'dies' there, then rises to a new loved life, with Christ at the centre. In this action, the candidate is able to slough off the old compromised self and reclaim his or her true identity, and thereafter leave wet footprints throughout life as proof of that baptism into Christ. Being forgiven is about being given a new relationship, full of abundant life.

We sometimes meet people who don't come forward to receive Communion and we might be puzzled. The reason is often that they don't feel worthy, which is tragic. The loving forgiveness of God is absolute; it only has to be received, not earned. This is one of the values of formal confession (Reconciliation of a Penitent), which is an underused pastoral resource available for a priest to use whenever the sheer objectivity of God's loving forgiveness is needed. Honest confession, followed by wise counsel and a clear declaration of forgiveness, can give enormous release.

Declaring forgiveness

This is the other dimension of forgiveness that crops up regularly in pastoral conversations and, sadly, in dysfunctional church relationships. It would be wonderful to think that the holy community of the redeemed would enjoy perfect harmony, but any church leader will tell of long periods of time spent trying to resolve relational disputes. 'Why can't we live differently?' is like asking, 'Why can't we cease being human beings?'

These are some of the principles that we need to remember in ministry as we encourage people to practise forgiveness.

It's tough and we need to salute and support those who manage it When it occurs between people, it has the feel of a miracle. In 2006, Charlie Roberts, a young married father who delivered milk to an Amish community, walked into a classroom and shot ten of the primary school-age girls sitting there, five of whom died and one of whom will always be in a wheelchair. He then shot himself. At his funeral, a group of Amish people fanned out to protect the killer's family from the media. They said to Charlie's mother, 'We're so sorry for your loss.' They had chosen the miraculous way of forgiveness.[2]

It's usually a process, not a once-and-for-all event It might be possible on some days and not on others, so we shouldn't expect a consistent attitude of forgiveness. Marina Cantacuzino of 'The Forgiveness Project' says:

> Forgiving is not a sign of moral or spiritual superiority but it's a journey, whereas revenge is a cycle. That journey isn't necessarily one way. People can forgive one day and not the next. It's a struggle for understanding, and it's difficult and brave.[3]

Because forgiveness is hard work, we need to respect the attempt, and offer support and encouragement on this very personal journey.

Forgiveness can't be required of another person And for some it proves impossible. When the Revd Julie Nicholson's 24-year-old daughter was killed in the London Underground bombings of July 2005, she found that she didn't want to forgive. She said:

> I will leave potential forgiveness for whatever is after this life. I leave that in God's hands. I have a certain amount of pity for the fact that four young people felt that this was something they had to do, but I certainly don't have any sense of compassion. Can I forgive them for what they did? No I cannot.[4]

This too needs to be respected. Fr Alois of Taizé says:

> There are situations where we don't manage to forgive. The wound is too big. We should remember that God's forgiveness never fails, but as for us it's sometimes only by stages

that we succeed. The desire to forgive is already a first step, even when that desire remains engulfed in bitterness.[5]

Forgiveness is a one-sided gift It has to be premature or it's not really forgiveness. Jesus didn't say on the cross, 'Father forgive them – if they apologize.' Forgiveness doesn't wait and see but, instead, takes the initiative and leaves the response to the other. This is a hard move to make when we're so used to negotiated transactions and contracts to sort out our problems, but that's the nature of grace.

Forgiveness is for the forgiver's own good The study of forgiveness has become one of the hottest fields of research among clinical psychologists in the USA where more than one thousand studies on the subject have been published in the last five years. Much of the research focuses on the health benefits, both psychological and physical, of forgiveness.[6] Forgiveness is good for us. A Chinese proverb says, 'Whoever opts for revenge should dig two graves.' The point is that forgiveness reverses the process of vengeance – which merely perpetuates the cycle of violent thoughts and actions – and it brings about a new freedom and a new possibility in relationships.

Our ministry in this tangled and sensitive area is both a responsibility and a privilege. When people entrust us with some of their darkest emotions, we have to remember always to be bearers of good news and grace. Jesus had hard words for judgementalism. But encouraging the giving and receiving of forgiveness feels as if it's taking us to the heart of the gospel.

Tailpiece: two stories

One of the most famous and notorious photographs from the Vietnam War was of Kim Phuc as a young girl fleeing naked from her napalm-bombed village. Her face, a mask of horror and pain, touched a generation. She is now a Christian and believes forgiveness helped to free her from her pain and anguish. She said, 'Even though so much of my body was burnt, my feet weren't burnt, so I could run out and be there for that photo. It saved a lot of souls and brought an end to the war.'

At the South African Truth and Reconciliation Commission, a white soldier and a black woman came together. The man had taken away and killed her son, and later he did the same with her husband. When the facts had been recounted, he asked the woman for forgiveness and she replied:

> You are asking for amnesty. I am asking for three things. You dragged my son out of bed and took him away and killed him. I want to be taken to the place where he was necklaced, and where his body is buried, so that I can pay my respects to him. You took away my husband and I never saw him again. I want to be taken to the place where he was shot, so that I can see where it happened and pay my respects. You have therefore taken away my whole family and I have no one to give my love to, so I want you to become my son, and come and drink tea with me once a week.

He did.

Resources

Stephen Cherry, *Healing Agony: Reimagining forgiveness* (London: Continuum, 2012).

Church House Publishing, *Common Worship: Reconciliation of a Penitent* (London: CHP, 2010).

The Forgiveness Project (<www.theforgivenessproject.com>).

Desmond Tutu and Mpho Tutu, *The Book of Forgiving* (London: Collins, 2014).

G
God

If it seems presumptuous to speak (or write) about God as if we know the answers, that's because it is. St Augustine said that anything we can understand cannot be God. But speaking about God is what clergy and lay ministers, and indeed all Christians, do. It's our job and our privilege, and it might well be what people are interested in. How can we believe in God? What does God do in the world? What kind of God can we believe in today? These are fundamental questions that any thinking person is almost bound to address at some stage.

Moreover, what we believe about God affects everything else we do in ministry – the way we pray with a dying person; if we preach, the way we speak about miracles; if we lead worship, whether we do so with an 'other-worldly' or a 'this-worldly' emphasis. It emerges in the way we offer pastoral care, the way we relate to the community and so on.

To sharpen the importance of the God-question even further, the clergy are inevitably visible witnesses and 'signs' of God wherever they go, particularly if they're wearing clothes that mark them out as clergy, whether attending an official function, travelling somewhere by train or buying an Americano in a coffee shop. Simply wearing a cross is a big statement today.

The social context

In a society where over half the adult population say that they have no religion, we have to be sensitive to the difficulties people have with the One we gladly worship. Our task isn't to badger people into belief but to point in wonder to the God who is at the centre of our lives. In fact, we often find a professed agnostic or even atheist is more open to a sensitive explanation of who we believe in than we might imagine. Douglas Coupland, author of *Generation X*, wrote in another book:

Here is my secret: I tell it to you with an openness of heart that I doubt I shall ever achieve again. My secret is that I need God – that I am sick and can no longer make it alone. I need God to help me give, because I no longer seem capable of giving; to help me to be kind, as I no longer seem capable of kindness; to help me love, as I seem beyond being able to love.[1]

There's a wistfulness in many an unbeliever.

We also need to be aware that, for many people, the very word 'God' carries much freight, even for Christians. It may have been used to load guilt on to people or fear. It may incite dislike, even hatred. The well-known atheist Richard Dawkins wrote:

The God of the Old Testament is arguably the most unpleasant character in all fiction: jealous and proud of it; a petty, unjust, unforgiving control-freak; a vindictive, bloodthirsty ethnic cleanser; a misogynistic, homophobic, racist, infanticidal, genocidal, filicidal, pestilential, megalo-maniacal, sadomasochistic, capriciously malevolent bully.[2]

It may be that we have to choose our words carefully and, if the word 'God' is too heavily weighted with negativity, speak of 'the divine presence' or 'the infinite source' or some other formulation, when referring to God.

We also need to be mindful that God proves elusive for many faithful Christians too. Former certainties slip, complexities of belief arise, boredom takes hold and passion leaks away. A congregation on Sunday morning isn't a gathering of people with clear convictions and one-hundred per cent commitment; it's people with a mixture of faith and doubt, people hungry for God and groping in the dark, people lost in the love of God and others whose faith has faded to grey. We have to be wary of making assumptions.

What do we *not* mean by 'God'?

Our task as Christians is often like ground clearance when we're talking with others about God. A good question to a non-believer can be, 'What do you mean by the word God?' If they attempt an answer, they may then be surprised when we say that we don't believe in that kind of God either. For example, we might say any of the following.

We don't believe that the existence of God can be definitively proved God is no-thing and can't be laid out on a mental dissecting table for analysis. God isn't one object in a field of objects; God is the source, ground and meaning of all objects. In spite of wonderful and suggestive arguments made through the ages, you can't make a watertight argument for God and finish with QED. It's like Harry Potter being asked to prove the existence of J. K. Rowling; it's impossible because they're in different orders of reality. As the philosopher Kierkegaard put it with disarming simplicity, 'God does not exist; he is eternal.'

We don't believe that God is somewhere else, doing something else, occasionally popping in to do some godlike thing, but generally absent We believe, rather, that God is always present, as present as the air we breathe, as present (and elusive) as the ocean is to the fish. It's not God who is absent; it's us, unable to be still enough and attentive enough to recognize the echoes of eternity. However, the image of God as a dominant, external power, working through control, submission, uniformity and coercion, dies hard. The alternative is God as love, mystery, unity, relationship and justice, working through freedom, mutuality, possibility and interdependence. This is the universe that I recognize and the God I seek to know. But the arbitrary, interventionist God hangs around in many human hearts.

We don't believe that God is like us, only bigger The tendency to anthropomorphize God is ever present. We can't easily conceive of love beyond what we see of it in a loving person, nor personhood beyond a particular person, nor a ground of being beyond and beneath the people and things we can see and touch. But such is the God beyond God, not an unreliable, tetchy, all-too-human god like those of the Greeks and Romans, but an ultimate creator of beauty and mystery. That word 'mystery' is often misunderstood too. There are two types of mystery: those where there's a puzzle to solve when enough information has been gathered and those where you say, 'The more I know, the more I find I don't know.' The latter is the nature of God.

What do we mean by 'God'?

This is where only the foolish dare to tread. There's a long tradition in theology that claims we can never say what God is, only what God is not. But because we haven't learned that lesson thoroughly enough, history is littered with partial or inadequate understandings of God. Nevertheless, we can give it a go.

God is the one unlimited reality that contains and includes everything which exists I realize that this definition of God is a bit like describing a kiss as 'the coming together of two pairs of lips for the reciprocal transmission of microbes and carbon dioxide', but it's a careful starting point. It avoids the trap of seeing God as a being within a field of other things and other 'beings' that exist as discrete entities. It avoids images of dominance and control, and it avoids suggesting that God is like us, only bigger. It suggests that God is the one true original. God had no reason to exist. Being God isn't a job; God wasn't appointed or 'made'. God just is. 'I am who I am' (Exodus 3.14). But in that ultimate mystery is room for a thousand astonishments.

Only metaphors will do when we talk about God We're so far out of our descriptive comfort zone that we have to scramble for metaphors and images, accepting that even these will be but pale attempts at adequacy. Some have already been mentioned – divine presence, ultimate source, unlimited reality – but the best may be the simplest. Mark Oakley writes, '*Love* is the only metaphor for God that should be pursued relentlessly.'[3] Such a metaphor has the merit of also being biblical (1 John 4.8) and it embraces the necessary qualities of relationship, freedom, mutuality, sacrifice and joy. It's a well-known teaching of the mystics that God cannot be thought; God can only be loved. Another simple biblical metaphor is that of *father*. It could also be mother, for God is beyond gender, but the same qualities are honoured as for love. We will each find images that speak best for us, but we will do well to offer a diversity of ideas to those we talk to, in order to give them a range of possibilities. Elise Fletcher, interviewed in the *Church Times*, spoke of her understanding of God as 'a diverse, creative, grace-filled Spirit who I couldn't describe but [is] ever present and full of possibility.'[4] I could go with that.

God is both ultimate and intimate It's important that we bear in mind both ends of the spectrum that in previous ages have been called transcendent and immanent. Our discourse about God probably veers between the two, depending on the nature of the conversation, but both are necessary as correctives to the other. The scale of God who holds in being our universe and whatever other universes there are, is beyond comprehension, yet this same God is our intimate companion, lover and guide. The problem lies in the middle ground between these two extremes of the ultimate and the intimate reality of God. This is the realm of the day-to-day God of both Sunday and Monday, who accompanies us every step of the way and who we increasingly try to recognize in everything that goes on. But it's also in this middle ground that we create our idols, the God we each want as our own possession, made in our own image, one we can try and control in prayer and by good works. Sadly, this is the middle-ground version of God that often features in our church discussions. We must push on to the God beyond God, the God deep within and the God in between, who we can find in everything.

God is always active in every part of life, 'under-ruling' rather than 'over-ruling' The trouble with some of our understandings of God is that they can tend to look somewhat static. The mathematician-theologian Blaise Pascal was protesting against this in the note that was found sewn into his coat after his death, saying, 'Fire! God of Abraham, God of Isaac, God of Jacob. Not the God of the philosophers and the scholars . . .' The God of divine fire is indeed always at work in every part of life, drawing all creation and all human endeavour towards the good, and the fulfilment of creation's potential. If we have to use a human analogy, God's gracious action works from the inside out rather than the outside in. God doesn't stand aloof from anything but is, by God's very nature, in the thick of everything. Our task is to recognize, keep up, and cooperate.

Quick idea: brainstorming about God

Invite people to do some hard thinking about God. Brainstorm the words and images that come to mind, without censorship – probably father, creator, king, shepherd and so on. Discuss the strengths and weaknesses of those images.

Strengths: biblical, powerful, reassuring, well established.

Weaknesses: do they mean much to today's young people? Do they emphasize the all-mighty at the expense of the all-vulnerable? Are they too anthropomorphic and make God seem like one of us, only bigger?

Invite people to write down quietly some other words and images that might communicate more meaningfully today (ultimate reality, underlying sustainer, overflowing source, generous love, gentle persuader, shimmering presence). Try starting with a noun and then adding an adjective. Compare and discuss. What are the implications for the language of our worship, our teaching and our evangelism?

How to relate to God

As God's agents, we're more often trying to help people encounter God than understand who God is. Arguments and discussion will have their place in nurture groups, apologetic talks and school discussions, and those are very important in a post-Christian society. Our task, however, is more likely – and more helpfully – to be encouraging people to leave the often dry river-bank of conventional religion and wade into the waters of the great river. This is where the divine Spirit is pouring through the world, bringing life to all who are willing to get wet. Jesus' concern was not to get people to believe correctly, behave correctly or secure eternal salvation; it was to invite people to live his way of love by immersing themselves in the vitality of the Spirit and the abundant life of the kingdom of God.

The fundamental assurance that we can have in our thinking about God is that we are made for him and can know each other because 'like knows like'. Our ministry is therefore best directed towards helping people realize that relationship. This means encountering *the God beyond* in worship (see **Worship)** and *the God within* in prayer (see **Prayer)**. Hopefully, we will also encounter *the God between* when we gather in community (church) to worship God for the sake of the world. It's in community that we recognize the face of Christ in one another and the necessity of seeing that divine image in the last, the least and the lost – and, indeed, in every person who comes our way.

Ultimately, it isn't ideas about God that matter. It's joining Jesus in the water.

Tailpiece: two classic statements about God

God is within all things but not enclosed, outside all things but not excluded, above all things but not aloof, below all things but not debased.

(St Bonaventure, 1221–1274)

God loved us before he made us, and his love has never diminished and never shall. The greatest honour we can give Almighty God is to live gladly because of the knowledge of his love.

(Julian of Norwich, 1342–c.1416)

Resources

Andy Bannister, *The Atheist Who Didn't Exist: Or the dreadful consequences of bad arguments* (Oxford: Lion Hudson, 2015).

Rob Bell, *What We Talk about When We Talk about God* (London: HarperCollins, 2014).

Marcus Borg, *Days of Awe and Wonder: How to be a Christian in the twenty-first century* (London: SPCK, 2017).

G God

Timothy Keller, *The Reason for God: Belief in an age of scepticism* (London: Hodder & Stoughton, 2009).

Sara Maitland, *Awesome God: Creation, commitment and joy* (London: SPCK, 2002).

Aaron Niequist, *The Eternal Current: How a practice-based faith can save us from drowning* (New York: Penguin Random House, 2018).

Keith Ward, *The Evidence for God* (London: Darton, Longman & Todd, 2014).

Rowan Williams, *Tokens of Trust: An introduction to Christian belief* (Norwich: Canterbury Press, 2007).

H

Holy Communion

One of the immense privileges of ordained ministry is to preside at Holy Communion or to take the sacrament to others. Sharing bread and wine is what Christians do when they get together. It's the central, defining act of a Christian community. And in an amazingly diverse set of circumstances, it simply 'works'; it makes the reality of God's presence come alive for people.

This was vividly put decades ago by Dom Gregory Dix:

> Was ever command so obeyed? For century after century, spreading slowly to every continent and country and among every race on earth, this action has been done in every conceivable human circumstance. Men have found no better thing than this to do for kings at their crowning and for criminals going to the scaffold; for armies in triumph or for a bride and bridegroom in a little country church; for the wisdom of the parliament of a mighty nation or for a sick old woman afraid to die.

Dix carries on with example after example, then he concludes,

> And best of all, week by week and month by month, on a hundred thousand successive Sundays, across all the

parishes of Christendom, pastors have done this, just to *make* the holy people of God.[1]

In more recent times, we could add that, on 20 July 1969, when the Apollo 11 space capsule landed with the first men to walk on the moon, the first thing Buzz Aldrin did when he and Neil Armstrong landed in the space capsule was to take Communion, so the first liquid ever poured on the moon and the first food eaten there were consecrated bread and wine.

As clergy, lay ministers and congregation, we are regularly in close contact with this bread and wine. Week by week it feeds us, paradoxically, by making us hungrier – for God. Through this bread and wine, God comes to us, so that we may come to God, 'in whom all our hungers are satisfied'.[2]

So what's going on, and how shall we share the significance of this profound activity?

Communion takes us back to the Last Supper and the key events of our faith Astonishingly, at that last fellowship meal with his friends, Jesus broke bread with those he knew would break fellowship with him. This was the night when the community disintegrated. It ushered in the terrible wreckage of the cross on Good Friday and the sensational beauty of the resurrection on Easter Day, the core truths on which the Church has fed ever since. But Jesus didn't leave us a creed or a set of beliefs; he left us with things to do and a way to live. He left us with bread and wine on a table and a towel on the floor.

The early Christians noticed that Jesus had a characteristic way of sharing special meals. He did it with the five loaves and two fishes, with which he fed over five thousand people; he did it at the Last Supper with his friends. He *took* the bread and wine in his hands, he *gave thanks* to God for this good provision, he *broke* the bread and he *shared* the food and drink with his companions. These four actions have been at the heart of the

Eucharist ever since. Jesus knew as well as anyone that people don't remember a set of beliefs as well as they remember distinctive actions. Here, then, was the life of Jesus, taken, blessed by his Father, soon to be broken on the cross, but then shared with the world for ever.

How could the disciples forget what he did that night – an acted parable of his life, death and new life? They didn't forget, and nor has the Church.

We take Communion because we need it We are often bewildered seekers, chased to exhaustion and desperately in need of something more sustaining than the thimbles of sustenance our shallow society offers. Rowan Williams puts it this way:

> We take Holy Communion not because we are doing well but because we are doing badly. Not because we have arrived but because we are travelling. Not because we are right but because we are confused and wrong. Not because we are divine but because we are human. Not because we are full but because we are hungry.[3]

At some level, many people realize that being part of a Peter Pan and Tinkerbell culture, wanting us to stay forever young and feed on superficial entertainment, just isn't enough. We need something more solid and sustaining. We Christians also know that we can't live on an unhealthy diet of fast food and easy answers. The bread and wine of Communion is the Christian answer to the unbalanced diet society offers to a hungry world.

Communion enables us to be more aware of Christ's presence in every place By recognizing Christ's presence in the bread and wine, we're helped to recognize Christ's presence throughout the week in everything that happens around us. It's mildly irritating when people ask Christ to 'come into' a situation or even to 'be present with us'. Where do they think he has been all this time? Christ is always present; what's missing is our recognition of him. Christians have different understandings of how Christ is present in the bread and wine but what matters is that he is. This recognition puts him at the centre of everything we do, both in the service and in the week that follows. We become more aware of the companionship of Christ and his love. We become more aware of what he's doing and what he's inviting us to join in with, for the sake of the world.

The Eucharist communicates beyond words Just as Jesus didn't burden his disciples with long, worthy explanations when he broke bread, so we find that Holy Communion speaks to our hearts at a deeper level than mere words can do. The point of a sacrament is that it's an outward sign of a larger mystery. When words fail because they're poor, thin things that can't carry profound truths, sacraments do the job for us. How can we stuff the deep mystery of an infinite God into the straightjacket of human words, words that have been chewed so often they've lost their taste and their meaning?

Sometimes we desperately need symbols, sacraments and silence to cope with enormous wrong. The Dominican Timothy Radcliffe was in Rwanda at the tail end of the atrocities in 1994. He saw the utter misery of the refugee camps and a prison that was like an abattoir, and a hospital where one child had lost both legs, an arm and an eye through a landmine. By the end of the day, he was traumatized. He wrote:

> That evening we celebrated the Eucharist in the sitting room of the [Dominican] sisters. The walls were filled with bullet holes from the recent fighting. When the time came to preach a sermon I had no words for all that I had seen. I had never met such suffering before. But I did not have to say anything. I was given something to do, a ritual to perform.

We re-enacted what Jesus did on the night before he died. We repeated the words, 'This is my body, given for you.' When we utter words of utter anguish, then we remember that on the cross Jesus made them his own. And when we can find no words at all, not even to scream, then we may take his.[4]

Sunday morning in our churches is nothing like this, but the principle is similar: the Eucharist communicates beyond words. I once asked a family with two young children what brought them so faithfully to the early morning Communion, and the mother replied, 'That service – it's a ball of fire.'

Quick idea: a teaching Eucharist

Warn the congregation that next week there will be teaching about the significance of the Eucharist as we go through the service. Then at obvious points in the service (for example, after the Gathering, before the Collect, in the sermon, at the Preparation of the Table, before the Dismissal) the president, preacher or another person can explain what's going on, why it's done as it is, where some of the prayers come from, and what it all means for the life of the believer. It might well need to be done over two weeks. The response of the congregation is likely to be one of appreciation as they discover why we do various things and how deep the significance of them truly is. They're likely to enter the service in future with greater relish and enthusiasm.

Communion is radically egalitarian and a model of social relationships We are all equally welcome, we sit at the same table, we eat the same food, we belong to one another and Jesus is at the centre, eating with sinners (us). When we come to Communion, we are figuratively – if not physically – gathered in a circle around the table of the Lord, and if you can visualize that, it means that we're looking at one another *through* Christ. We see one another as brothers and sisters loved and fed by the same Jesus. No one can claim any superiority of wealth, class or status. We're on level ground and we all belong to one another because we all belong to Christ. 'Because there is one bread, we who are many are one body, for we all partake of the one bread' (1 Corinthians 10.17).

This is a really exciting reframing of relationships in a society that's so blighted by inequalities. We're modelling a just society. And it has implications right the way through the life of our own churches, from the question 'Who sits where?' to 'Who makes the decisions?'; from 'Who do we consult?' to 'How do we spend our money?'. When we truly put Jesus in the middle, all sorts of things begin to look different. 'Am I my brother's keeper?' (Genesis 4.9). Yes, I am.

Communion looks forwards to a new heaven and a new earth This is a foretaste of the heavenly banquet when all things will have been gathered up in Christ (Ephesians 1.10). The consecrated bread and wine can be seen as symbolizing the new creation to which all history is heading. It's a new world in miniature. Theologian Harry Williams put it this way:

> Just as finally in the new heaven and the new earth Christ will fill all things, so now, in anticipation of that divine act of renewal, he fills the consecrated bread and wine. They do not cease to be bread and wine. They do not change into something different from themselves. But when first brought to the altar they belong to the present world in which nature is not yet fully or finally gathered up in Christ, [but] then as the service proceeds, they are *transferred* into the new world where nature, recreated, is in the fullest sense the Body of our Lord Jesus Christ because he fills it wholly and it is gathered up fully in him.[5]

Holy Communion, therefore, looks both backwards, to the central acts of the life, death and new life of Jesus, and it looks forwards, to the new world that Christians claim we have already entered through our relationship with Christ. That is why we want to emphasize the importance of Communion. It's not a mere act of remembering what Jesus did; it's actually about *participation* in Christ, being united with him, taking the life of God into our own lives and locating our lives in him. It's union or, as orthodox Christians describe the Eucharist, it's 'life, light and fire'.

One way to think about this is that, when we go up for Communion, we raise our hands to receive and we carry in those hands the joys and burdens of our lives and of our week. Here are the things done and not done, the anxieties that we carry, the people in our hearts, the tasks ahead, the issues no one else knows about. They're all here, offered to God, and, in exchange, wonderfully, God gives us the life of Christ, here in this bread and wine, and we go out to offer that life of Christ, now afresh in our own lives, to the particular world we inhabit with all its relationships and tasks. What an exchange – my life for the life of Christ. When we come back down the aisle, I fear we often look very serious. Yes, it is a serious thing we've done, but I sometimes wish we could smile a bit more with the joy of that exchange. After the wedding of Prince William and Kate Middleton, a verger was caught on camera doing a cartwheel. That would do just fine.

The role of the clergy and lay minister

My experience of presiding at the Eucharist is that I feel I'm on the edge of something huge that I can't actually pin down. The whole of the experience is greater than the sum of the parts. Thomas Merton wrote that when presiding, 'I feel washed in the light that is eternity and become one who is agelessly reborn.'

Whether we are presiding, administering or taking Communion out to people in the community, we are stewards of a gift that's immensely precious to people and, therefore to be handled by us not casually but 'reverently, discreetly, soberly and in the fear of God'.[6]

All of us who come to Communion are participating in that four-fold action of Jesus. We offer ourselves to be *taken, blessed, broken open* and *shared* for the sake of the world. We break open the love of Christ latent within us and share it with those we meet in the week. We have to do that in detail, in *this* action, with *this* person, and in *this* moment. It's a love that flows from *this* table.

Tailpiece: out of the mouths of babes

A few years ago, at mass, I was sitting near a woman who had a small boy on her lap. He looked to be about three years old. It was an ordinary Sunday mass and the child seemed like an ordinary child. At the time of consecration, the faithful were quiet, the bell was rung, the priest held up the sacrament and everything was as expected. Then the child, who had up to now been quiet, shouted out: 'Hello Jesus!' He dragged out the hello into one long yodel, 'Helloooooooo'. Everybody in the church turned. Like many children he knew he had an audience when he had one, so he lauded out the louder, 'Helloooo Jesus!'

It was a moment of delight. The priest looked shocked, blank, as if Jesus had turned up in actual flesh and bone. Theologically, of course, the child was deliciously correct. The woman holding the small boy looked mildly embarrassed but mostly thrilled. I cannot remember anything else from that mass apart from the warm welcome of a small child who took the story seriously.[7]

Resources

Jonny Baker, *Curating Worship* (London: SPCK, 2010).

Paul Bradshaw, *Companion to Common Worship* (London: SPCK, 2001).

Stephen Burns, *Liturgical Spirituality: Anglican reflections on the Church's prayer* (New York: Seabury Books, 2013).

Mark Earey, *Liturgical Worship* (London: Church House Publishing, 2018).

Benjamin Gordon-Taylor and Simon Jones, *Celebrating the Eucharist: A practical guide* (London: SPCK, 2011).

Michael Perham, *New Handbook of Pastoral Liturgy* (London: SPCK, 2000).

The Iona Community, *Iona Abbey Worship Book* (Glasgow: Wild Goose Publications, 2017).

I

Identity

The letter 'I' invites a chapter on Identity but this is mostly covered in the chapters on Self-care and Vocation.

You could, however, reflect on the importance of being able to answer three questions on identity.

1 'Who am I?' Just as it's immensely reassuring to see the red arrow on a map in a strange city that says 'You are here', so knowing where we are in relation to God and the world can be deeply helpful and give us a firm grounding for ministry as Christians. Jesus was enabled to embark on his ministry after he had been baptized and heard the glorious affirmation of his Father saying, in effect, 'You are my child, my beloved, and I'm thrilled to bits with you.' As Christians we can be assured that God says the same to us. Paul tells a group of early Christians confidently, 'You are hidden with Christ in God – and Christ is your life' (my translation of Colossians 3.3–4). This is who we are and where we are.

2 'Who am I if I've taken on an official position in the Church?' Some people are subsumed by their role. They seem to lose themselves in the trappings of an authorized ministry or the responsibilities of an official role. We have to guard our humanity first of all and make sure we remain the unique person God has called, resisting the temptation to inhabit some idealized version of the role we now have. The best person to ask about this is your life partner or best friend; they'll tell you if you've lost the plot.

3 'Who will I be when I retire?' What will be left? The transition from active ministry into retirement or the end of a term of office, can in some cases be quite traumatic. For this reason, it's important to know that:

- we are Christians before we are occupants of a role;
- we have planned what we'll do next; and
- we continue to sink deep roots into God.

Resources

Francis Dewar, *Called or Collared: An alternative approach to vocation?* (London: SPCK, 2000).

J
Jesus

'J' could hardly be for anything else, could it? Jesus is the heart and soul of our faith, the one around whom our lives as Christians revolve. Our church life needs constantly to land on Jesus at the centre, and our own lives need to be conformed steadily to his life, the gold-standard for humanity.

In one sense Jesus lived on the edge of history, in a distant outpost of an irritating corner of a great empire, but in another sense, history was reframed around this man. H. G. Wells wrote, 'I am a historian. I am not a believer. But I must confess, as a historian, that this penniless preacher from Galilee is irrevocably the centre of history.'

This is a handbook on ministry, not a book on theology, so the purpose of this chapter is to examine how we let the story of Jesus impact our ministry. Essentially, our task is to direct people to Jesus. Here is the key person, the man of full and final significance, in a faith we both believe in and try to live out. The stakes couldn't be higher.

Michael Mayne, former Dean of Westminster, wrote:

> Christianity is not about the trivia of our lives; it's about
> their ultimate purpose. Either what it claims touches our

very centre and profoundly changes the way we see everything – or it is a comforting but ultimately irrelevant story
that changes nothing. For if God was not in Christ and
our faith is a delusion, then we are born into a chancy and
precarious universe with no ultimate purpose or destiny.
But if Christ was in very truth the window onto God then
we are held in being in our lives and through our deaths by
that loving, creative Spirit whom he taught us to call Father,
and who has created us to know and love him, even as we
are loved and known.[1]

Jesus is the heart of it all.

So in what ways does the story of Jesus shape our ministry?

Apologetics

In a society where conspiracy theories abound, it's not surprising
that we often find we have to discuss whether Jesus really existed
or did any of the things attributed to him. A Church of England
survey in 2015 found that 40 per cent of the 4,000 people ques-
tioned didn't believe Jesus was 'a real person', and 25 per cent of
18–34-year-olds believed he was a fictional character. We may
have to make the point that whereas, for example, there are no
written references to King Arthur until three or four hundred
years after he is supposed to have lived, the earliest letters about
Jesus were written within twenty-five years of his death and the
Gospels were appearing only fifteen years later. Moreover, the
Jewish historian Josephus wrote about Jesus around AD 93, and
twenty years later the Roman politicians Pliny and Tacitus wrote
about the annoying followers of Jesus they had to deal with.
Strikingly no one in the ancient world seemed to have ques-
tioned whether Jesus really existed.

We may also find ourselves deep in discussion about whether
the Gospels are reliable, and some accessible books on this
are listed in 'Resources' below. It's sufficient here to say that

the Gospels were dependent on oral tradition, which was the normal way of holding memory in that culture, and that the Gospels therefore came from the first generation of Christians, those who could have corrected errors from their own first-hand witness.

Discussion may also focus on what we mean by maintaining that Jesus was both human and divine. It sounds paradoxical – but then paradox is a very important category in a world trapped in binary thinking. We say that Jesus was God's self-portrait, his autobiography or the playwright stepping on to the stage. One writer put Jesus' divinity this way, 'In Jesus God was saying, "I am like this, and I am *so* like this that, as far as you are concerned, I *am* this."'

Nevertheless, Christians will have different understandings of what 'this' is, in terms of his divinity. At one end of the spectrum there will be those who make full-blooded statements such as those of the Nicene Creed, that Jesus is 'God from God, Light from Light, true God from true God, begotten, not made'. Here, Jesus Christ is the second person of the Trinity, eternally God, existing before creation itself. This is unashamed 'top-down' Christology. At the other end of the spectrum there are those who see Jesus as the man who was completely aware of God's presence in his life, and who was fully responsive to that presence moment by moment, thereby obeying God's will and demonstrating God's way. He was the ultimate human being who lived so close to God that people who knew him well found themselves saying that the best description of him that they could come to was that he was 'the Son of God'. This is clearly 'bottom-up' Christology.

It can be helpful in discussion to offer this range of top-down or bottom-up approaches to the nature of Jesus, and to recognize that we all place ourselves somewhere on the spectrum between the two. Who are we, in any case, to saddle Jesus with the limitations of our puny brains? And who are we to tell others what they must think? We are there to help, suggest, open doors and both ask and answer questions.

The apologetic task was never more needed than in our post-Christian society. Conversations can be struck up anywhere and it's important to have some clear arguments available as we continue to point people to the Prince of Life.

Evangelism

Outside the Church there's a dearth of knowledge about Jesus. The 2015 research project for the Church of England, 'Talking Jesus', two-thirds of adult Christians polled said they had had a conversation about Jesus with a non-Christian in the last month – a surprisingly high figure. However, of the non-Christians who had had such conversations, forty-two per cent said they were glad not to share the Christian's faith, and, sadly, two-thirds said they now felt more negatively about Jesus.

Something is going wrong. However, Jesus remains the best offer a Christian can make. Here is a life of such quality, defined by love and the pursuit of peace and justice, that few (you would think) could resist the opportunity of a relationship with him. We have to tell the story well. We have to purify it of the unnecessary accretions of time and tradition, and like a freshly restored painting, present Jesus in all his attractiveness. It's often said that the Church is only one or two generations away from extinction. If we stop telling the story, it will disappear.

We need to tell the story in schools, where Open the Book has proved to be so popular (see 'Resources' below). We need to tell the story in Christian Basics and other nurture courses. We need to tell the story in the media, especially social media. We need to tell it in art, film, poetry and music. Above all, we need to tell the story in how it has impacted on our lives, where our life story has been touched and turned by the story of God's love. It's all possible. It just takes courage and natural enthusiasm for the things that we value most. (For more on this see **Evangelism**.)

Justin Welby set a great example as Archbishop of Canterbury by making it a rule that he would never have a conversation with anyone in a significant position in society without speaking in some way about Jesus. A Church of England report that came to General Synod in 2019 said that,

> If one additional person in fifty from our regular attenders invited someone to a church event and they started attending, it would totally reverse our present decline. Nationally the Church would grow by 16,000 people per year, offsetting the current net loss of 14,000.

Of course, the hard part would be to persuade the fifty not to leave it to the other forty-nine!

Quick idea: faces of Jesus

Collect a range of different images of Jesus, easily found on the Internet or from favourite paintings, cards, books and so on. Make sure the selection includes images from different cultures and others that challenge our easy assumptions. Put them together as an on-screen presentation or, if no more than about ten, on a single A4 sheet. Invite people in twos and threes to identify which ones they respond to most, positively or negatively, and why. Then, together, ask people to offer their responses, drawing out the value of each one or the reason why Jesus might have been depicted in that particular way. The ensuing discussion or teaching should broaden and deepen people's understanding of the central figure of our faith. (See 'Resources' below for the excellent book and CD Rom *Seeing our Faith*).

Discipleship

Jesus is the touchstone of our ministry in developing disciples. The goal of Christian maturity is that we become Christlike. It's not *knowing* everything about Jesus; it's not *believing* everything about Jesus; it's *becoming like* Jesus. We'll never do it, of course, not this side of the Second Coming, but it's the essential journey we're on and it gives an exhilarating sense of purpose to Christian living. Although we never 'arrive' in this life, we always have to 'run with perseverance the race that is set before us, looking to Jesus' at the finishing line (Hebrews 12.1).

Formation as a Christian primarily involves looking to (at) Jesus. If we don't want to change, it's best not to look at Jesus for too long, because as we look at him, we become increasingly saturated in the love that looks back at us, and that's what undoes our resistance. We're opened up to grace. When the Curé D'Ars asked a poor farm worker why he sat silently in church for so long, the man pointed to the crucifix and said, 'I look at him, and he looks at me, and we're happy together.' We become like the one we look at. (That also applies of course to a culture mesmerized by wealth, fame, power and the addictive toys of a consumer culture. We become obsessed with what we look at.)

Jesus is the trailblazer of the life we were made for, so the formational task is to mould our life and values, our actions and behaviour, around what we see in Jesus. We need to present that possibility in all its attractiveness and excitement. There's nothing insipid about Jesus. He was a robust, purposeful and generous teacher, a wonderful communicator, a man of laughter and deep emotion, capable of great friendship but also of excoriating fire when he saw people being misused. He was wary of wealth and power but celebrated the abundance of God in what he did with water at a wedding, with bread and fish at a late lunch, and with forgiveness for a woman caught in an illicit fling. 'He never called the poor lazy, never justified torture, never fought for tax-cuts for the wealthiest Nazarenes.'[2] He wouldn't leave anyone behind, outside or forgotten. He was, in fact, a human being at peak performance. He is the one we want to emulate.

How do we do it? In all our small groups, in preaching, in mentoring, in talks, conversations and asides, we have to hold out this Jesus so that he dazzles us all. There are courses galore and the opportunities we have are immense. But we have to be intentional and give people the challenge – 'Do you want to be more like Jesus?'

Spirituality

This follows on naturally from discipleship and formation. We often speak somewhat lazily about having a relationship with Christ. Indeed, Paul often uses phrases such as 'I want to know Christ and the power of his resurrection' (Philippians 3.10); 'It is no longer I who live but Christ who lives in me' (Galatians 2.20). But what does that mean to a growing Christian? How can you know someone who lived two thousand years ago?

A spectrum of interpretations of that kind of phrase might help our conversations with those seeking clarity on what 'a relationship with Christ' might mean. At one end of the spectrum is the personal friendship with Christ that's the characteristic experience of the new Christian and of millions of mature believers worldwide. Jesus is known in prayer and presence, a daily companion and friend. Further along the spectrum is knowing Jesus as the compelling figure who lived in Galilee, challenged the norms of established religion, died tragically and rose astonishingly, and has both disturbed and enchanted the world ever since. This is the enigmatic teacher and prophet with whom we struggle and celebrate, but ultimately with whom we want to align our lives. At the far end of the spectrum is a more tangential understanding of knowing Christ, for Christ here is a loving, teasing, elusive divine presence in our lives. We might think of an 'atmosphere of Christfulness' around our lives, a more spiritual, opaque perception of Christ. Many of us could identify with all three of those positions on the spectrum, but it can often help people if we outline these possible stances.

But whatever understanding we have of Christ's presence with us, we're inviting people to leave the dry banks of conventional religion and to wade into the water of God's great river. We're inviting them to swim, copying the style of Jesus. The river has many names: it's the eternal current, the way of Jesus, the kingdom of God. But the essential move is away from observing religious activity from the river bank and getting into the fast-flowing stream, using our muscles to swim with the current. This is the spiritual challenge. Swimming will involve using many different muscles (see **Bible**, **Mission** and **Prayer**) but let's not delude ourselves that this move from the river bank to the water is not one of the main challenges of our ministry. The river bank is often crowded; observation is easier than participation in the Christian life. But if we stay on the river bank too long, it becomes seductive and we easily fall asleep.

> **Tailpiece: quote from Archbishop Justin Welby**
>
> At the Last Judgement God isn't interested if I was Archbishop of Canterbury. He couldn't care less. He's interested in whether I put my trust in Jesus Christ.[3]

Resources

Kenneth Bailey, *Jesus through Middle-Eastern Eyes: Cultural studies in the Gospels* (London: SPCK, 2008).

Bible Society, 'Open the Book', storytelling programme (<www.biblesociety.org.uk/get-involved/open-the-book/>).

Bruce N. Fisk, *A Hitchhiker's Guide to Jesus: Reading the Gospels on the ground* (Grand Rapids: Baker Academic, 2011).

Michael Green, *Lies, Lies, Lies: Exposing myths about the real Jesus* (Nottingham: IVP, 2009).

Janet Hodgson, *Seeing our Faith: Creative ideas for working with images of Christ* (Norwich: Canterbury Press, 2011). With CD Rom.

J. R. Porter, *Jesus Christ: The Jesus of history, the Christ of faith* (London: Duncan Baird, 2007).

John Pritchard, *Living Jesus* (London: SPCK, 2010).

John V. Taylor, *The Christlike God* (London: SCM Press, 1992).

Peter J. Williams, *Can We Trust the Gospels?* (Wheaton, IL: Crossway Books, 2018).

K
Kingdom of God

The kingdom of God has to be at the heart of our ministry as Christians because it was the key content of Jesus' teaching. It was his constant central message and offered a new liberating framework for religion both then and now. Mark 1.14–15 gives the clearest, most succinct description of his message: 'Now after John was arrested, Jesus came to Galilee, proclaiming the good news of God, and saying, "The time is fulfilled, and the kingdom of God has come near; repent and believe in the good news."' That is to say: the time is now, the kingdom is here, change how you approach life. At the centre of those three phrases the actual content of the message is the kingdom.

When Jesus went back to see his family in Nazareth, having set up home with Peter's family in Capernaum, he preached a dynamic sermon in the synagogue, quoting Isaiah 61 as his manifesto for a new order. It was good news for the poor, release for captives, recovery of sight for the blind, and the year of the Lord's favour (Luke 4.18–19). He expanded on this royal charter in the Beatitudes in the Sermon on the Mount. *This is why he came*. It wasn't just to 'save souls'; it was to proclaim a new world order that he called the kingdom of God.

Jesus then constantly illustrated what that meant. His parables repeatedly started 'The kingdom of heaven is like . . .' (see, for example, Matthew 13). He approached his central theme from a variety of angles and used a wide range of everyday images (seed, a lost coin, buried treasure, a fine pearl, a fishing net, a wayward son) but always the image of the kingdom of God (or of heaven) was set before his hearers as the gift that he uniquely brought.

Our task, therefore, as followers of this kingdom-Jesus, and as ministers among his people, is constantly to describe and illustrate what it's like to be part of this kingdom. In myriad ways, we're inviting people to enter this kingdom, explore it, and live out its values.

What do we mean by 'the kingdom'?

In some ways, of course, the word 'kingdom' is an alien concept. It's not a word in regular use today and, at its worst, it could be seen as patriarchal and oppressive. Undeniably, when God spoke on Mount Sinai or when Jesus spoke of his Father's sovereignty, it doesn't sound like democracy as we know it today. It might be easier to speak of the reign of God or the arena in which God's ways are made real. The kingdom exists wherever God's will is cherished and obeyed, whether that be in a person, an activity or a social reality. Jesus cut the ribbon on the kingdom. He taught, demonstrated and embodied the kingdom of God. In short, Jesus *was* the kingdom, visible in action.

Just like Jesus, in ministry we're constantly trying to both illustrate and demonstrate the values and dynamic of the kingdom, and so we too try to find adequate ways of describing what we most deeply desire. I mentioned the royal wedding sermon of Bishop Michael Curry in the chapter on **Care and compassion**. He was experimenting with different words for the kingdom when he suggested this:

Imagine a world where love is the way. Imagine our homes and families where love is the way. Imagine neighbourhoods and communities where love is the way. Imagine governments and nations where love is the way. Imagine business and commerce where this love is the way. Imagine this tired old world where love is the way. When love is the way, then no child will go to bed hungry in this world ever again. When love is the way, we will let justice roll down like a mighty stream and righteousness like an ever-flowing brook. When love is the way, poverty will become history. When love is the way, the earth will be a sanctuary. When love is the way, we will lay down our swords and shields, down by the riverside, to study war no more. When love is the way, there's plenty good room – plenty good room – for all of God's children.[1]

That's a pretty fair description of the kingdom of God. It's a big picture of course, but you wouldn't expect God's vision to be anything less. It's the big picture of how things should, and could, really operate. Most people want their lives to have significance and be part of a larger framework of meaning and purpose. We want something more than our small lives being soft, overfull and passive. Jesus' invitation was to a larger field of significance and purpose, and he called it the kingdom of God. Our invitation ultimately in ministry, alarming as it may sound, can be no less.

Distorted versions of the kingdom

Too often the Church has offered sub-standard versions of the good news of the kingdom. Here are some, in exaggerated form. The kingdom is about:

- sin management and an evacuation plan. On this account, the good news is about dealing with our multiple wrongdoings. Our problem is personal sin, but Jesus died for us and his death does away with our guilt, so we can be rewarded with heaven as our eternal destination;

- behaviour modification and a self-help programme. We get into a mess in all sorts of ways, but Jesus has given us new laws to obey and the Church is here to encourage or enforce them. Certain standards are necessary to continue to carry a membership card for the Christian club;
- 'God will fix things for me.' It's rarely put as crudely as this but there is a belief going around that if I do right by God, jump through the right hoops, believe the right things and behave the right way, God will make sure bad things don't happen to me. A close relative of this belief is another: 'Everything happens for a reason,' so, if things go wrong in my life, I must have stepped off the golden path, a belief that has caused untold emotional and spiritual damage.

It's noticeable that in these parodies-with-enough-truth-to-cause-alarm the reference point for the good news is always personal. It's another version of the 'Big Me' problem of our society where everything is about my personal welfare and well-being. Our churches are inevitably contaminated too.

Let's look at a healthier understanding of the good news of the kingdom in both its social and personal dimensions.

The social reality of the kingdom of God

Jesus announced and inaugurated a new social order that was and still is a clear alternative to the way of violence, exclusion and self-centredness that prevails in so much of our world. It's the reign of love, peace and justice, in the constant near presence of God. Jesus gave us glimpses of what such a reign looks like in the Sermon on the Mount and in his parables and teaching, but he didn't try to offer us a systematic account of the Statutes, Constitution and Memorandum of Association of the kingdom. He gave us glimpses of the kinds of things it meant, the kinds of ways we would live and the kinds of ways we would interact in the community of the kingdom.

One of the great things about God is his subtlety. God gives us snapshots to entice us. God isn't 'in your face' all the time with irrefutable instructions and demanding timetables. In Christ, God gives us a map of the territory of the kingdom, along with compass, walking boots and a packed lunch, and says, 'Go and explore'. And, as Dutch theologian Abraham Kuyper memorably said, 'There isn't a square inch in the whole domain of our human existence over which Christ, who is sovereign over all, does not say: This is mine.'[2]

This comprehensive coverage of life is our mandate as Christians to work out what kingdom values mean when applied to the 166 hours of the week in which we are not in church. Teaching, homegroups and conversations have to break out of their captivity to church life and address the complex issues people face at work, at home, in friendship groups, personal finance, cultural pressures, addictive temptations and so on. Sermons need to tackle politics, science, sex, loneliness and the everyday struggles we all face. The church bubble is a dangerously seductive place in which to linger, but that won't hasten the coming of the kingdom.

Moreover, and crucially, we are called to be kingdom builders wherever we have influence. God's goal is a healed creation, a new world order in which the common good, social justice, and peacemaking are the hallmarks. How then can we nudge the organizations, institutions, systems, families and relationships in which we are all involved, in the direction of the kingdom? This is the challenge we have as people of God in season and out of season. How is what we're doing on Sunday impacting on what we're doing on Monday?

Quick idea: kingdom spotters' map

Obtain or sketch a map of the community around your church. Invite the group to do some 'kingdom spotting', that is, to mark on the map any places where kingdom-building is going on. These activities are ones where, as above, the common good, social justice and peacemaking are in evidence. People should be able to identify organizations, charities, local authority provision, innovative schemes and entrepreneurial projects that exhibit the marks of the kingdom. They won't all be Christian ventures, although there will be Christians involved in nearly all of them. Discussion might revolve around the inclusive scope of the kingdom, the ways and generosity of God, and the role of the local church in all that's going on in the community.

The personal reality of the kingdom of God

After looking at the social reality of the kingdom, let's look at the personal implications of adopting the kingdom as our reference point.

I love maps. I can spend hours devouring the contours, the place names, the distances, the high points. I delight in planning walks I'll probably never do or in revisiting sunlit days of my youth walking blue remembered hills. But looking at a map is nothing like walking over the terrain it represents. If I never get out into the countryside, I've rather missed the point.

It's too arrogant to say that many church-goers have rather missed the point, because people come to church for wonderfully diverse reasons and it's not for us to quibble, but it's nevertheless true that in our churches in the West there's a lot of map-reading and not quite as much walking and climbing as we might like. We want to get people on to the hills!

It's the difference between looking at a bottle of wine and sipping a glass of it, between studying a scorecard and being at the match, between watching the river and wading into it. Belden Lane writes, 'There are two doors in the next life – one is labelled "heaven" and the other "lecture on heaven". Everyone in the West is lined up outside the second door.'[3] While this is an exaggeration, it's true that our early experiences of religion are only preparing us for the immense gift of being, in some way, burned by divine fire. Those of us in ministry are charged with the responsibility of offering people holy tools to go deep with God. This may be where we start talking about the Jesuit Examen, about lectio divina, centring prayer, practising the presence of God, Ignatian meditation, the Jesus Prayer, a structured office, praying with nature and more (see **Prayer**). We start offering ways of serving others that put faith into practice outside the holy house. We talk about God truly living in us, and us in God; and we encourage the confidence that when the Word is read and the sermon preached, there really will be a word from the Lord, and God really will speak to us.

The difference between observation and experience in the Christian faith was summed up for me when a lovely, humble Christian woman was anointed by the river Jordan and said afterwards, 'Nothing happened, and everything changed.' That's what we work for in ministry, that people will find in their faith that nothing new happened (same place, same service, same people), but that everything changed and God's love is now delivered daily, freshly baked in the ovens of their own experience.

Can the Church be an expression of the kingdom?

Yes and no. Yes, as long as we know we'll never succeed in completing the task. As we know, the world is divided into different time zones so that new year in Australia happens half a day before it happens in the UK. In a related sense, the kingdom of God belongs to 'new time', resurrection time or a new world. We still live in 'old time', a world still suffering from miserable compromises, but as Christians we have the incredible privilege of living in both time zones at once, with the task of trying to bring 'new time' values and priorities into our 'old time' society and culture. We live in the confidence that the kingdom of God has arrived and we are part of it now.

The Church can be a (flawed) expression of the kingdom as we can try to be a laboratory of the future kingdom where we inevitably make lots of mistakes but nevertheless have occasional breakthroughs as we experiment with projects that belong to 'new time'. We can try and co-create experiences of beauty and truth through worship, art, music and other means that might attract people to the kingdom we so lovingly commend. We can challenge injustice both in the near community and in wider society as we increasingly see the world through the eyes of Christ. And we can pursue personal holiness, not as selfish ambition but as purposefully aligning ourselves with Christ. These are all proper kingdom projects for those of us in the Church. So the Church can indeed be a partial expression of the kingdom (on a good day with a following wind), but it's definitely not the finished product.

We can believe in the Church as long as we believe more in the kingdom, and we can belong to the kingdom as long as we believe most of all in the King.

Tailpiece: receiving the kingdom of God

Jesus said that 'whoever does not receive the kingdom of God as a little child will never enter it' (Mark 10.15). Here's a story of a child who had received the kingdom without knowing it.

A little girl was suffering from a rare form of blood disease. Her only hope was to receive a blood transfusion from someone with exactly the same blood type as hers. After testing various members of the girl's family, it was discovered that her ten-year-old brother had a precise match. The doctor talked to him and gently raised the possibility of his providing a transfusion for his sister. 'Your sister is dying,' he explained, 'but your blood would be able to save her. Are you willing to give your blood?' The boy hesitated for a moment, and the doctor saw that he was anxious at the prospect.

But the lad agreed to the process. After the transfusion the doctor went to visit the brother to see how he was. 'Tell me,' implored the boy, 'how long until I die?' Only then did the doctor realize his young patient's misunderstanding and know that he had been willing to give his life so that his sister might live.[4]

Resources

Malcolm Brown (ed.), *Anglican Social Theology: Renewing the vision today* (London: Church House Publishing, 2014).

Aaron Niequist, *The Eternal Current: How a practice-based faith can save us from drowning* (New York: Penguin Random House, 2018). Contemplative activism.

John Pritchard, *Living Faithfully* (London: SPCK, 2013). Money, sex and power.

Jim Wallis, *On God's Side: What religion forgets and politics hasn't learned about serving the common good* (Oxford: Lion Hudson, 2013). Faith, politics and the common good.

Tom Wright, *God in Public: How the Bible speaks truth to power today* (London: SPCK, 2016). How the Bible speaks to power.

L

Leadership

In this chapter, I'm focusing on the leadership offered by clergy and lay ministers, but much applies equally to leaders of study groups, pastoral groups and others. See what fits.

Jesus has to be our exemplar as a leader, but clearly he led in a very different context from ours, so we shouldn't try to 'read off' principles of leadership too closely. We can certainly look for inspiration and wisdom from him, but probably not for techniques. But neither should we succumb to the plethora of secular books in the airport bookstore that promise us instant success in dynamic leadership. A few volumes have come through and proved themselves valuable to the Church (see 'Resources' below), but the 'holy society' of the Church is not the same as a FTSE 100 company whose goal is shareholder profit.

Jesus' approach was essentially one of mentoring. He worked hard with the twelve, the ragged bunch of disciples in whom he invested so much time and effort. He gave them seminars on what was happening around them, he debriefed them on the parables, he gave them individual and small group tutorials, he sent them on mission and he took them on retreat. So there's huge poignancy in the fact that they all disappeared at his time of crisis – a lesson for leaders still.

If mentoring was Jesus' main method of leadership, the clearest teaching he offered is found in Matthew 20.20–28, culminating in his challenge, 'Whoever wishes to be great among you must be your servant, and whoever wishes to be first among you must be your slave; just as the Son of Man came not to be served but to serve, and to give his life a ransom for many.' Leadership here is about service, modelled on a life given away not in teaspoons but in handfuls.

It's impossible in such short compass to encapsulate the wisdom of countless Godly leaders through the centuries. Instead, with apologies, I offer the top ten principles I've found helpful as I've seen them in others and tried to follow. The first three are foundational.

> ### Quick idea: coaching
> Make enquiries about whether there's anyone around, in the congregation or beyond, who has been in a coaching position and would offer their time and experience free of charge. Such people exist. A coach asks accurate questions, listens carefully to the answers we give and reflects those answers back to us, usually in written form after the session. We are therefore not being pushed in any direction but rather enabled to hear what we are really saying. The result is that our thinking is clarified and our decision-making better informed.

Ten principles of church leadership

1 God must fill our vision If we don't have the compelling mystery of God as our number one obsession, then why should anyone else be bothered? God is our constant point of reference, the One with whom we begin and end every day, and in whose sight we are perennially loved. We have to face the danger that in our role as leaders we can become so caught up with the things of God, the paraphernalia of religion, that we lose the divine enchantment of our faith. If we don't sustain the sacred centre of our lives, we could become perfectly competent religious functionaries, but not much more. When I became an archdeacon I realized that I knew quite a lot about the Bible, public worship, church practice, pastoral ministry, church law and finance, and even (God help me) the Church Representation Rules and the Pastoral Measure – so I could do this job *almost entirely without reference to God*. I had sufficient experience for the job and a modicum of skill, but here lay disaster, an abyss. A fundamental reset of the compass was necessary – nothing should be done without God as true north. Leaders in the Church must have God front and centre in heart and mind.

2 *In leadership, character comes first* Jesus scored highly on this one! One of the classic triads of interviewing is that we look for competence, character and chemistry, and that middle quality, a character of integrity, openness and trustworthiness, is absolutely vital. The writing of a good CV is an art that can be taught, but what matters isn't so much a good CV as a good person. If a congregation recognizes these qualities then anything is possible. Without them, the relationship will at best limp along and at worst it will crash and burn.

3 *Leaders must have emotional and social, as well as spiritual, intelligence* They aren't just good in themselves but 'good with people'. No one comes into leadership in ministry with a full palette of colours. However, being able to relate well, warmly and constructively with people is a red line if ministry together is to thrive. Those who are withdrawn, stubborn or lose their temper are not going to be popular. Someone who bullies, demeans, is rude or fails to encourage is going to be avoided. Those who are self-absorbed, narcissistic or miss crucial pastoral needs have already set narrow limits to the effectiveness of their ministry. The bottom line is that we have to love people and demonstrate that love in the way we listen and respond to them (see **Attentiveness**). Try reading 1 Corinthians 13.4–7 as a template and compare your style of relating to people with that masterpiece of sensitivity.

These are the other seven principles.

4 Leadership is itself led by vision In ministry, the clergy and lay ministers – with as many others as possible – have to address the big picture issues, and to do this they have to keep a wide-angle lens on their vision. We want to see as much as possible and to do that we need others around us who see what we don't see. A wise approach to discerning an overall vision and subsequent understanding of mission has four phases.

- *Listen* to the people of God (in particular those we usually screen out) in order to hear the voice of the Spirit.
- *Shape* what we hear into a workable strategic framework.
- *Articulate* the vision and strategic framework to the whole church – and then articulate it again and again.
- *Enable* the delivery of the mission prayerfully and strategically.

In this process we have key questions to ask ourselves about any prospective action: 'How does this fit with the kingdom of God?' 'Do we sense Jesus is in this?' 'What are the values underlying this work?' 'What is the impact of this likely to be, for whom and for how long?' 'How does this fit with other priorities in mission?' If our heads drop to small things in seeking God's vision for our church, there's a well-known biblical warning, 'Where there is no vision, the people perish' (Proverbs 29.18 KJV).

5 Leadership is dispersed throughout the Church Leadership is essentially corporate. Strong, individualistic leaders may attract others through their charisma but they're often heading for a fall because God has formed his Church into an entire body of many different talents, and this applies to the local expression of the Church as well as the body corporate (1 Corinthians 12; Ephesians 4). We need to work in teams, groups and working parties, recognizing that no one is ungifted. It's wonderfully liberating when we're in a group and find that a previously quiet member of the congregation comes into their own at a certain stage and quite naturally slips into modest leadership. In this way, we listen to one another, draw wisdom from one another, learn and shape together, and get the task done. A good mantra might be 'high trust, high support': trust to the hilt a group of the right people, then support them to the maximum, rather than leave them to it with the risk of them floundering. Leadership is all around; it's just that we may not recognize it. Look and be expectant.

6 A good leader is committed to the well-being of everyone in the church – and of the Church as a whole It can be helpful when meeting anyone in the course of ministry to be aware, naturally, of our own needs and agenda in the meeting, but also to have as a question at the back of our mind, 'How can I help this person to flourish?' Too often church leaders with busy lives and many agendas, see a church member as a potential peg to put into an empty hole, without thinking too deeply about whether the peg is square and the hole is circular. We have to start with God's view of the person as a treasured individual, both gifted and fallible, looking to the church for particular reasons and resources. The question then is, 'How can we both give to and receive from this child of God?' We also, as leaders, need to have an eye on *the overall health of the church*, to see where it might be weak or undernourished, where it's outgrowing its strength or needing a rest. We have to see the whole elephant, not just the foot, the trunk or the tail. We need to look out for temperatures rising too high and be ready to cool things down before conflict breaks out. We have to teach that difference in the church isn't a design fault; it's God's gift of diversity in his people. But if there is substantial conflict, there are skilled resources available to help. Our concern is for the well-being and flourishing of the whole body and all its members.

7 *Effective leaders admit mistakes and learn from them* A favourite cartoon of mine shows a disconsolate woman trudging up a mountain following a man pushing a full supermarket trolley. The caption says, 'Having insisted this was the way back to the car, Paul is unable to admit that he is wrong.' Some church leaders are the same. Others, happily, recognize when they've made a mistake, apologize properly and change course. I learned much from my supposed 'sacking' of the choir when I was a vicar, although decades on I'm still not sure I apologized as I should have done.

8 *Allow for the creative possibilities of mess and be prepared for the death of some parts of church life* Ministry is irrevocably untidy because human life is untidy. To expect a clear desk at 5 p.m. with every task finished, every pastoral problem solved and Sunday's sermon in the bag, is to live in fantasy land. Our lives are messy; we never seem to get on top of things; issues come in ungainly shapes and in multiples of three. Fine, now we can get real. Let's not expect the kingdom of God to arrive by next Friday. Along with this sense of untidiness and an element of failure comes the probability that the paradigm of death and resurrection will apply to our church life too. Some practices, groups and ways of doing things will outlive their usefulness to us and to the kingdom. Then we need the courage to say so and to arrange palliative care and a good funeral. We can leave resurrection to God; God has more experience than we do.

9 *Be a capable administrator* That isn't the same as '*be* the administrator'. That task should be for someone dedicated to that role. But we should be able to turn messages round with reasonable speed and to be properly prepared for worship, meetings or conversations. People get very frustrated when their clergy and ministers are habitually inefficient (one-off mistakes are usually forgiven). Bishops often hear words to the effect, 'We love him, of course – but . . .' And it can be a big 'but', denoting genuine irritation, rising to anger, at the sheer absence of care displayed in administrative chaos. I found it useful to think, 'inasmuch as you did it to one of these, my pieces of paper/emails, you did it to me.' (Compare Matthew 25.40.) Being capable at administration is part of good pastoral care.

10 Don't do it all! This is a plea for 'good enough'. The tasks of ministry are infinite; the only person who can make them finite is me. I have to know when to say, 'That's good enough in the time available and with the skill I have to bring.' Mind you, it can be useful to have some personal time-savers. A favourite of mine was 'worst things first'; if I got one of the most problematic things done first of all, everything else felt like a bonus and I'm sure that I was more efficient as a result.

Tailpiece: the Rule of St Benedict on leadership

The Abbot must hate faults but love the brothers. When he must punish them, he should use prudence and avoid extremes; otherwise, by rubbing too hard to remove the rust, he may break the vessel. Let [the Abbot] strive to be loved rather than feared. He must so arrange everything that the strong have something to yearn for and the weak nothing to run from.[1]

Resources
Jim Collins, *Good to Great and the Social Sectors: A monograph to accompany good to great* (Boulder CO: Harper Collins, 2005).

L Leadership

CPAS, 'Lead On' email service and 'Growing Leaders' course (available at:<www.cpas.org.uk/church-resources>).

Steven Croft, *Ministry in Three Dimensions: Ordination and leadership in the local church* (London: Darton, Longman & Todd, 1999).

Michael Green, *Radical Leadership* (London: SPCK, 2017).

HTB, Leadership Development, (<www.htb.org>).

Keith Lamdin, *Finding Your Leadership Style: A guide for ministers* (London: SPCK, 2012).

Patrick Lencioni, *The Five Dysfunctions of a Team: A leadership team* (Hoboken, NJ: John Wiley, 2002).

Iain McGilchrist, *The Master and his Emissary: The divided brain and the making of the Western World* (London: Yale, 2009).

Sarum College, Centre for Leadership Learning (<www.sarum.ac.uk/learning/leadership-ministry>).

The Internet is full to bursting with leadership material, as are most bookstores. Select with care.

M

Mission

Mission is all-embracing. It's what we do as a Church and it's what all ministers, lay and ordained, are there for. As such, it commits us to the most exciting agenda imaginable – the transformation of the life of the world under God. All ministry is concerned with taking further that glorious goal, even on a wet Wednesday in January. It's the sum total of the Church's task in relation to the world, and it ought to inform and shape everything that we do in ministry.

Missio Dei

This is the well-known theological category that all of us engaged in authorized ministry have been taught. It reminds us that God's character is fundamentally missional. Mission is God being true to God's nature. God is constantly pouring love into the world to make, remake and complete it, and our task is to cooperate with that great enterprise. It isn't sufficient to say to a church leader, 'We've got all these things to do already – and now you expect us to do mission as well!' No, mission is what we're about.

This mission of love is embodied and expressed in the life, death and new life of Jesus Christ. Jesus both opened the door to the kingdom of God and showed what living under the reign of a loving God would mean. In this way, we get our bearings in mission from Jesus because he exemplified and made real the outpouring of God's love into the world. He emptied himself so completely he ended up on a cross.

It's this theology that animates the Church but can seem so very different from 'Christianity-as-going-to-church.' The gap shows how far we've fallen as a Church from the high theology of mission that clergy learnt in training. Putting it technically, Christology should lead to missiology, and that, in turn, should lead to ecclesiology, but so often in practice we reverse the order so that we attend to the Church's internal concerns before the great vision of mission or the even greater vision of Christ. Theologian D. T. Niles said, 'We don't really understand what it means to be a missionary church until we realize that what Jesus is doing isn't collecting Christians but renewing creation.'

The mission of the Church is the mission of God – to transform lives and communities so that they reflect the values of the kingdom. We look for the transformation of our lives in surrender to Christ, but also for the transformation of society, our politics, our banking and legal systems, international relations, media, the arts, the Church. This is not a modest agenda. But it starts small and local, in people motivated to change tired, unjust systems – people energized by the love of God.

The Anglican Lee Abbey Movement was once setting up a missional community and it declared that the task of the community was to 'move in, live deep and share everything (especially the gospel).' That sounds remarkably like what Jesus did.

The Five Marks of Mission

This is now the classic statement on mission with which many churches work. All lay and ordained ministers know it and sometimes it percolates further into church life more widely. The Anglican Consultative Council first put forward this understanding of mission in 1984, with the addition of wording on peace and reconciliation in 2012.

- To proclaim the good news of the kingdom.
- To teach, baptize and nurture new believers.
- To respond to human need by loving service.
- To seek to transform the unjust structures of society, to challenge violence of every kind and to pursue peace and reconciliation.
- To strive to safeguard the integrity of creation and sustain and renew the face of the earth.

These are sometimes shortened to: Tell – Teach – Tend – Transform – Treasure.

In those five marks, we cover evangelism, growth in discipleship, pastoral care, social and political action, and environmental commitment. The mission of the Church is to anticipate the reign of God and to test it out as well as we can in our current context. We're working towards the transformation of the life of the world under God.

If that seems too remote a goal for the average churchgoer, it might help to start from much simpler questions about recent actions. For example, we could ask questions such as these about each mark of the mission.

To proclaim the good news of the kingdom Have we mentioned Jesus in any context recently? Have we told someone we'd be praying for them? Have we talked about church to someone who doesn't go?

To teach, baptize and nurture new believers Have we given encouragement of any kind to a newcomer at church? Have we spoken to a new parent about baptism? Have we helped with Open the Book at our local school? Have we prayed for particular children in our church?

To respond to human need by loving service Have we taken a friend who's facing a problem out to coffee? Have we visited, written to or phoned someone who's been bereaved recently – or taken round a meal? Have we bought a copy of the *Big Issue* and talked to the seller for a while? Have we supported a charity?

To seek to transform the unjust structures of society, to challenge violence of every kind and to pursue peace and reconciliation Have we signed an online petition on a particular social injustice? Have we actively supported an asylum seeker locally? Have we prayed about a world situation and not just in a church service? Have we tried to calm anyone down or mediate in a disagreement?

To strive to safeguard the integrity of creation and sustain and renew the face of the earth Have we recycled everything we can in our area? Have we promoted or supported green policies in our own church? Have we examined the carbon impact of our travel? Are we careful with water usage and endeavoured to reduce how much electricity and gas we use at home?

These kinds of question can demystify the grand-sounding goals of the Five Marks of Mission and be the springboard to a deeper engagement with them. People often feel helpless or run themselves down; we need to affirm, encourage and build confidence that we all matter and can all do something.

A working model

The five marks give a linear account of the nature of mission. Images are often more effective in making their point, and one such image for what mission might mean in the local church is that of a swimmer's breaststroke. Bear with me on this! It's helped many churches to understand God's call to them and to explore the strengths and weaknesses, and the opportunities and priorities of their mission. Pictorially, it looks like this:

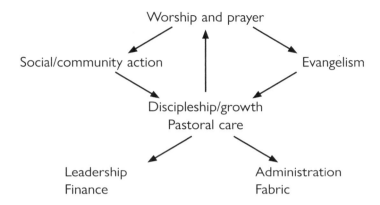

M Mission

Worship and prayer

Social/community action

Evangelism

Discipleship/growth
Pastoral care

Leadership
Finance

Administration
Fabric

Worship and prayer

The old Westminster Confession asserts boldly that the chief purpose of men and women is 'to worship God and enjoy him for ever'. This then is the forward thrust of the arms in the breaststroke; it sets the course and it identifies the direction. This means that in order to inspire and resource Christians well for their mission, worship must be thoughtful, rich, imaginative and memorable. It's our chief and glorious task and must never become routine. Prayer is the oxygen of the Christian life and we want to offer timely help to anyone looking for the most satisfying and enriching ways to pray 'their way' – which won't necessarily be our way. Our storeroom of prayer needs to be full and regularly restocked, in order to offer the right help at the right time.

Social and community action

To get moving in the breaststroke, the arms need to work hard, pushing back the water and propelling the swimmer forward. Caring for the well-being of the community in which we're set is key to following Christ in mission. We aren't a religious island in a sea of secularity; we are communities of principle, with love and justice written into our DNA, seeking to serve the common good. It can be useful to sharpen the question about our place in the community by asking, 'In what way are we making a difference to the community around us?' This might help us to identify the particular gift we can offer, not seeking to duplicate what anyone else is doing but perhaps using our premises, our willing volunteers or our capacity to bring people together. People usually won't take us seriously until they see how seriously we take them.

Evangelism
This can be where people quietly tiptoe off the stage. It's so awkward, so embarrassing and so open to mistakes. But it's so necessary. It's the other sideways thrust of the swimmer's arms that moves the swimmer forward. If we only activate one arm (social action), we go round in a circle. We need to balance it with the awkward imperative of evangelism. We have a gospel of dazzling grace. Once we've recognized the scent of that grace, we're forever checking around for signs of its presence. But when it comes to engaging with the world beyond the Church it often seems that the biggest question we're asking is, 'Will you give us some money to help pay for our new roof?' There's a mismatch here; we have a life-giving secret but we don't want to talk about it. For some answers, see **Evangelism**.

Discipleship and pastoral care
The swimmer knows the direction and the arms are working hard to give impetus to the stroke. But what is needed now is for those arms to come back into the body, so that the swimmer's strength is built up and ready for the next stroke. In terms of our model, this represents those activities that are necessary to maintain and grow the strength of the Body, the Church – and this equates to discipleship and pastoral care. Discipleship means focusing on our growth towards maturity as Christians through teaching and learning, and all activities that broaden

and deepen our faith. At the same time, there's need of pastoral care for those who are living in the shadows, both in the church and in the wider community. Wherever we look there are wounded veterans of life's mischances and the Church is never more Christlike than when it comforts and heals. See **Care and compassion**.

Leadership and administration

The swimmer's legs and feet, meanwhile, are kicking away to maximize the forward movement. Without that energy, the feet (and eventually the whole body) would steadily sink. Without good leadership and effective administration, the Church too will flounder (see **Leadership**). The other leg is vital too. This is *finance* and *fabric*, the resources needed for a church to function and to have a good, safe, warm and accessible environment in which to meet.

The model isn't perfect, but it serves to identify the main functions of a church in mission. The image might help the church council or a church awayday or weekend to focus on its task and to review its strengths and weaknesses, with a view to resetting priorities.

Quick idea: thinking about mission

To stimulate thinking about mission, attach long and wide sheets of paper (or a continuous roll if you can find one) to the wall of the room, and divide the available white space into as many decades of the life of the Church as seem relevant (perhaps four or five). Work with the group to identify major events in the nation and wider world over those decades, writing them on the paper in large-size marker pen. This gives a perspective and activates memories. Then follow a similar process identifying the major events and developments in the life and mission of the Church in the same decades. People enjoy their memories! Lead this into a discussion on what the priorities in mission ought to be for the next period. Point out that it's the next chapter in the same book, not a new book. The swimming analogy might help here or a SWOP analysis (strengths, weaknesses, opportunities, priorities).

Style in contemporary mission

Context is crucial in mission, as anyone who has been introduced to Vincent Donovan's *Christianity Rediscovered* (see 'Resources' below) will know. Our present context requires many adjustments to the style of our mission from what would have been effective in previous decades. Without going into detail here are some of them:

Questions, discussion and disagreements rather than answers, presentations and authority Social media, the blogosphere and a 24-hour information exchange mean that everyone feels entitled to a voice, and public discourse is conducted with a notorious disregard of old rules. Deference is out, and we have to adjust.

Events rather than programmes Experience is modelled for many today around memorable events rather than ongoing programmes that require continuous attendance. These events need to be imaginative and memorable.

Relationships rather than propositions Mission is a relational activity more than one based on believing particular doctrines and ideas. Belonging to a community of faith and having valued friendships is more effective than signing up to statements of faith.

'Gatherings' rather than conventional church Sunday church attendances may yet fall further, but small groups, large festivals and experimental communities will probably become more important. Authenticity will be paramount.

Inclusion rather than entry qualifications Our welcome needs to be unconditional. Border control and the assessment of fitness for entry is as counterproductive as it's bad theology. God doesn't love us because we're good; God loves us because God is good and wants us to share in that goodness and love.

Partnership rather than ownership The Church needs to look for partners in kingdom activity whether they have the right label or not. There's no room for claiming to be the one true pond. The kingdom is vastly bigger than the Church, and God is always looking for co-workers of any shape, colour or creed.

The Bible's Big Story, homing in on Jesus, rather than a pre-occupation with the Church The Big Story of the Christian faith is increasingly an alternative world-view that is strange and often intriguing to a post-Christian (but not post-religious or post-spiritual) society. Jesus remains the towering figure to whom we can confidently point.

Telling it slant rather than telling it straight Our approach to proclamation needs to be much more subtle and nuanced. The arts are a good friend here as they can bring people tiptoeing towards the divine through poetry, art, music, films, plays and novels.

Contemplative mission rather than triumphalist mission We need to do fewer things but do them better, and to look to God for God's own sake rather than to bolster our armies for an assault on the disbelieving opposition. Moreover, we need to look compassionately *with* God at this complex world rather than looking *to* God to sort out the mess for us. Let the vision of God fill our gaze as we bask in the compassionate gaze of God. In mission, our task is to enable a serious conversation with our culture about its beliefs, values and practices, seeking to draw society closer to the ways of the kingdom of God. It's a considerable task, but if God is who we believe God to be, why should we settle for anything less?

Tailpiece: the mission to go green

The church of St George, Wash Common, outside Newbury, felt called to become a fully eco-friendly and potentially carbon-neutral church as part of their response to the fifth Mark of Mission. The cost would be a million pounds. The project (completed in 2016) was divided into five phases and involved raising nearly half the money from internal church-giving and the rest from Government and Lottery funds as well as dozens of other bodies. It entailed fixing 129 solar panels on the roof (with feed-in tariff), insulating the large main ceiling, fitting underfloor heating, laying down insulation, putting in place a new efficient boiler and installing a ground source heat pump. The result is a genuinely green church providing a warm, welcoming and sustainable community space at the heart of Wash Common, and a church at the centre of the 'Greening Wash Common' initiative. Everybody wins.

Resources

Richard Carter and Samuel Wells (eds), *Who is my Neighbour? The global and personal challenge* (London: SPCK, 2018).

Vincent Donovan, *Christianity Rediscovered* (London: SCM Press, 1982).

Brian McLaren, *The Great Spiritual Migration: How the world's largest religion is seeking a better way to be Christian* (London: Hodder & Stoughton, 2018).

Graham Tomlin, *The Provocative Church*, 4th edn (London: SPCK, 2014).

Jim Wallis, *On God's Side: What religion forgets and what politics hasn't learned about serving the common good* (Oxford: Lion Books, 2013).

N

Narrative

If the devil has all the best tunes (actually, he doesn't), then Christians have the best stories. We have the Big Story of God's transformational love, from creation to new creation, and we have a multitude of stories of how God's people have lived within that larger narrative or fallen outside it or forgotten it. The power and prevalence of story is a huge gift to Christians involved in any form of ministry. A Jewish proverb says that two things are needed in winter – fire to warm the body and stories to warm the heart. We have stories aplenty to warm the heart, whatever the season of the year. Mark Oakley puts it neatly: 'God so loved the world that he gave us stories.'[1]

Here are some of the reasons that the category of story is so important for ministry.

- Our culture is soaked in stories. Wherever you look, we are being offered stories, whether it be in films, novels, small-screen dramas and soaps, YouTube uploads or even adverts. It's there in the way news stories are told or sporting events previewed. It's there in our conversations over dinner and catch-ups over coffee. It's there in the stories we read to our children from their earliest days, and in the stories we recall with our elders in their latter days. We're always listening to or telling stories.

- We are programmed to think in narrative. In the words of James Bryan Smith:

  Narrative is the central function of the human mind. We turn everything into a story in order to make sense of life. We dream in narrative, day-dream in narrative, remember, anticipate, hope, despair, believe, doubt, plan, revise, criticise, construct, gossip, learn, hate and love by narrative. In fact we cannot avoid it. We are storied creatures.[2]

- Relationships depend on the exchange of stories, whether that be with our children, our friends or people we are getting to know. It's particularly important for victims of trauma trying to get their bearings again. Counsellors and therapists spend their lives listening to stories and helping people make sense of them. Youth workers and community organizers live in a sea of often conflicting stories. Ministers spend their lives both listening to personal stories and telling the story of God, the ultimate 'divine comedy' that leads to a new heaven and a new earth.

- Communicators know how powerful a story is and how it can travel to places that mere facts hardly penetrate. Political communicators know how to tap into a deeper, underlying narrative that's scarcely even recognized by the people who live by it until it's put into a neat slogan: think of 'Yes we can', 'Make America great again' or 'Take back control'. These deep narratives are often much more influential than higher-level analysis and argument.

Story, then, is a very powerful category of communication and it's important that Christians recognize its importance and use it responsibly and constructively.

Narrative is important to ministry in at least three ways: in telling the story of faith, in understanding the Church we serve and in working with the Church and wider community.

Using narrative to tell the story of faith

Jesus was a storyteller. As Madeleine L'Engle put it, 'Jesus wasn't a theologian; he was God telling stories.' The Gospels record at least forty parables, his preferred teaching method. He didn't give us worked-out doctrines, complex creeds or confessions of faith; he told stories.

Our task, therefore, is to keep telling not only those stories but also Jesus' own story in his own way – which, of course, was not to hammer home some moral message at the end of the story but simply to let it lie and do its subversive work. It's worth spending time honing our skills in storytelling, and we should not assume that 'anyone can tell a story'. Anyone can, but not everyone can do it effectively. We need to improve our skills. Watch how stand-up comedians spin their stories of everyday life so mesmerizingly. Nor need we be restricted by a purist belief that we mustn't use any words or ideas that aren't in the Gospels. We need to use the 'baptized imagination' and bring the event to life. Say it, sing it, act it, dance it or put it into poetry, mime, film or social media; but in whatever way, make sure to tell it!

The urgency of telling God's story lies in the fact that as a culture we have largely forgotten it. The art historian Neil MacGregor puts the point well: 'In a sense, we are a very unusual society. We are trying to do something that no society has really done. We are trying to live without an agreed narrative of our communal place in the cosmos and in time.'[3] The Christian gospel has given Western culture that 'holding narrative' for centuries, but now it is either deliberately denied or carelessly forgotten. We have to keep telling God's story and the stories within God's story because, in religious terms, our culture is functionally illiterate.

Within that great umbrella, we also have to encourage the telling of our own stories and how they have interacted with God's story. This is the realm of testimony, of bearing witness to our own experience. The way our experience is understood and interpreted by others is their business, but the experience itself is sacrosanct – it's our story and no one can countermand it. Testimony at a confirmation or in any other setting, offered not by a 'professional Christian' but by an everyday believer, is very powerful for both listener and speaker. Hopefully, people in our churches will grow in confidence in answering the question: 'What has God been doing in your life recently?'

In Christian communication, narrative gets past our defences. Why did C. S. Lewis tell the Narnia stories? To get past the watchful dragons.

Using narrative to understand the church we serve
Here are two ways to do this.

World-view
James Hopewell, in his book *Congregation: Stories and Structures*,[4] used his skills as a social anthropologist to develop an approach to congregational life based on the stories members told of themselves and their life together. Through extensive research and 'participant observation' he found that churches would plot themselves somewhere on a square with four quadrants, that is, four categories that described their characteristic world-view. (The terms used are somewhat specialized and have other meanings elsewhere).

1 *Canonic*: where people rely on authority, either of the Bible or of tradition, to negotiate and sustain their beliefs and practices. We might see this in more conservative evangelical or Anglo-Catholic churches.
2 *Gnostic*: where people rely on processes that hopefully make for common understanding and harmony. This might be a description of many mainstream Anglican church congregations – nothing too revolutionary, steady-as-you-go.
3 *Charismatic*: where people look primarily to divine action and

the personal work of the Spirit. Open evangelical and charismatic churches may fit in this category.

4 *Empiric:* where people rely on evidence, data and common sense rather than any of the above. This tendency towards 'being realistic' is typical of some middle-class, professional congregations.

No church would fit neatly into just one of these quadrants through all of its members clustering together, but usually a majority of congregants would gather around some negotiation of the four spaces, with a few renegades dotted elsewhere.

Thinking about the corporate personality of the Church in this way (with a lot more subtlety than space here allows) enables us to see why congregations operate in certain ways and why they might resist certain changes or resent particular styles of leadership. We need to listen to the implicit world-view of the Church and together write the next chapter of the continuing story of the Church rather than try to write a whole new book.

Narrative ecology

In a chapter on 'narrative ecologies' Yiannis Gabriel develops a novel approach to understanding congregations, but again it is based on story.[5] He suggests congregations might be like:

- *narrative temperate regions*, where there is a profusion of varied stories and ideas, making it hard for leaders to plan or control;
- *narrative monocultures*, where only one dominant story is really acceptable and alternative stories are frowned upon (in an extreme form this can become a cult);
- *narrative deserts*, where perhaps there's a taboo regarding stories or connections between people who aren't strong enough for members to either tell or hear their stories;
- *narrative mountainous areas*, where there are only a few rather

feeble stories and no real energy for narratives (this might describe some Churches Together groups or deanery synods!);

- *narrative marshland*, where stories sink into the mud because, say, a working group has done a piece of work but it's been forgotten;
- *narrative jungles*, which are like temperate regions, only hotter and wetter, so things grow faster and wilder, and they may be more difficult or dangerous for leadership to work with; newer charismatic churches might experience this;
- *narrative allotments*, where people carefully collect and protect their stories and there's a preference for warm, loving relationships and the avoidance of conflict – and possibly not much room for new, challenging ideas.

This ecological image could be a good one to play with, and it might offer a church a common tool to help members understand what's going on in their life together and how to adjust their practices to be more effective and productive.

Quick idea: a storytelling workshop

This is a way of giving people greater confidence in telling their story of faith. Put people into pairs and give them five to eight minutes to tell each other a story from the last twenty-four hours. It could be something that happened to them, a story they read or heard, a dream and so on. Then ask them to tell a story of some significant happening in their primary school years, then secondary school. The event could be hard, humorous or just 'big', but one that in some way marked their life. Then try for a story they've heard, seen or read that has stayed with them through the years, one that they've repeated or tucked away as important to their way of thinking about life. It could be a true story or a fictional one, a major event or a marginal one, but one that in some way has stayed with them as significant. Finally, ask them to spend ten minutes each telling the story of their faith, how they started, how they grew as believers or how faith was challenged, the twists and turns of the journey, and where they are now. This is very often the most important story they have to offer to another person. It's the heart of evangelism.

Using narrative in working with a church and the wider community

Narrative has various effective uses in ministry, some of which are obvious, others less so. It helps to think about the following.

Know your story as a person and as a person in Christ As we grow in discipleship it's important to be aware of the influences that have shaped us and how the story of Jesus came to impact on our life. This story of ours is the gift we have to give to others when explaining or sharing our faith, so it's important to understand how it developed. We need to encourage that confidence in one another (see 'Quick idea' above).

Know the story of the Bible – the Big Story – and be able to relate the parts to the whole It's not unusual to find long-standing churchgoers for whom the overarching narrative of the Bible is still a bit of a mystery and who struggle to find their way around the Bible. Clergy and lay ministers should never miss an opportunity to show how the Big Story works in sermons, small groups, discipleship development, mentoring and so on (see 'Resources' below).

Know the story of our own denomination and what makes it distinctive For example, the Anglican Church came to define itself on the basis of its loyalty to Scripture, tradition and reason, mediated through personal experience and pastoral ministry. People are helped by knowing what makes them who they are and how they got there.

Know the story of the local church and how it came to value what it does and how it does it For the clergy, the first phase of any new ministry must be one of listening, listening and then listening again. We need the story of the church, told in many different voices, including, if possible, the voices of those outside the church. Alongside that, we need to learn the story of the wider community because we want to serve that community and help it celebrate (or lament) its defining events.

Listen to the stories people tell about themselves, their faith and their church These are precious narratives and require of us genuine interest, respect and confidentiality. When we are trusted with these stories, we can then point to appropriate help in people's onward journey, through opportunities to grow or serve, contacts to make, spiritual accompaniers and so on.

Listen to the stories of the future These are the hopes and dreams that are shaping the lives of individuals and of the church. As we do this, we're listening for what the Spirit is saying and gradually learning how to respond more accurately.

Tailpiece: the homeless girl

The young homeless girl spent a lot of time in the West End square, hoping to get into conversation with people. She didn't necessarily want money, she just wanted to be noticed, but people were usually too busy to pay her any attention.

One evening there was a movie premiere in the square. Crowds gathered, limousines glided up and cameras flashed. The star of the film eventually arrived looking impossibly glamorous in a stunning dress glimpsed through the extravagant folds of her rich cloak. She posed while the cameras clicked furiously and the adoring crowd pressed closer. The little homeless girl got more and more indignant. Eventually she worked her way through the crowd and under the rope, and stood defiantly by the glamorous film star. 'Look,' she said, 'this isn't fair. No one pays me any attention, when all I want is to be noticed and have some conversation, but when you come into the square in your gleaming car and posh clothes everyone goes wild and can't take their eyes off you!'

'You're right,' said the glamorous film star. 'That isn't fair. Why don't you come with me in future? I could carry you in the folds of my cloak.'

'I'd like that,' said the little homeless girl. 'What's your name?'

'I'm called The Story,' said the glamorous film star. 'What's your name?'

'I'm called The Truth,' said the little homeless girl.

And from that time on The Truth went around wrapped up in the folds of The Story.

Resources

Andy Frost, *Long Story Short: Finding your place in God's unfolding story* (London: SPCK, 2018).

James F. Hopewell, *Congregation: Stories and structures* (London: SCM Press, 1987).

Vaughan S. Roberts and David Sims, *Leading by Story: Rethinking church leadership* (London: SCM, 2017).

Gerd Theissen, *The Shadow of the Galilean* (London: SCM Press, 2010).

For children

Bible.org, *Walk Through the Bible* (<www.bible.org.uk>).

Bob Hartman, *Rhyming Bible* (London: SPCK, 2019).

Vaughan Roberts, *God's Big Picture* (Downers Grove, IL: InterVarsity Press, 2009) (available online at: <www.clayton.tv/find/explore/1272/0i0/2924/>).

O
Older people

Our churches are not short of older people. What we mean by 'older' is, of course, an open question. As far as most of us are concerned, it's about fifteen years older than we are ourselves. With life expectancy rising there's no need to agree with Truman Capote that 'Life is a moderately good play with a badly written third act.' There's plenty of vigour in most retirees and many years of active enjoyment of life lie ahead.

There are many benefits to this. One is that the normalization of two parents working at least part-time means that the value of grandparents in childcare is enormous. The average age at which people become grandparents is around fifty, with thirty-five years of being a grandparent to come. Another benefit is the availability of a reservoir of time, experience and wisdom that many voluntary organizations rely on, including the Church.

Hopefully, churches will see this pool of talent as a huge gift. Not all are wise, however. One person, after enthusing about his church's youth programmes was asked how it reached older people. 'What would be the point,' he replied. 'What would they bring?' Ageism is alive and well in churches too.

We also have to be aware that healthy longevity is something of a middle-class benefit. How long we live depends on our relative affluence because lives are cut short by poverty. The 'silver pound' may be widely spent on cruises, weekend breaks and National Trust cream teas, but others are left with few assets and poor health after forty years of hard work and worry. And in a culture spinning ever faster, some older people are thrown off the edge, with loneliness as their unwelcome guest.

The church has an important ministry with older people, both rejoicing in their gifts and alleviating their difficulties. What are the principles that might guide that ministry?

Principles of ministry with older people

Ministry is always 'with' and not 'to' Older people often aren't accorded the respect that many cultures used to give them and where, in the context of the extended family, they were seen as the repositories of wisdom and experience. To be young, active and beautiful has become society's favoured template, so that getting older is seen principally in terms of deterioration and decline, and to reach real old age is to fall off a cliff. The Church needs to be different and to reflect a biblical respect for old age.

Retired people offer enormous resources of time and experience, and all have gifts The actor Ralph Richardson was sometimes seen on all fours in the wings of a theatre saying, 'Has anyone seen my talent? I know I had it. It was quite small, but very shiny.' The church needs to recognize and rejoice in those small, shiny gifts.

Older people are not homogeneous There is a danger of older people being seen as a single group – the grey-haired backbone of the congregation. In fact, the variations are as great as at any other stage of life, depending on outlook, wealth, upbringing, education, personality type, health, stage of faith and so on. There is no such thing as a typical 'older person.'

There can be much mutual pleasure in relationships that skip a generation Parents may be the ones who take the flak and grandparents the ones who get the benefit. Outside the family, this can translate into a variety of intergenerational activities with schoolchildren and older people working together on remembered life-stories, memory cafes, mentoring and simple friendship.

Older people can be crucial change-makers The elderly are not usually opposed to change on principle. It's casual change, change which seems to be for its own sake, that can raise hackles. When change is well thought-out and clearly explained, older people can be a great asset in the process of managing change. They don't feel their life depends on it and they have a clearer view of what really matters. Older people can have a significant influence in swinging a congregation round to a new course of action.

Basic comforts and facilities in church are important, such as food, warmth, transport and access Accessibility is an expression of the hospitality of God so it really matters that wheelchair ramps are in place, noticeboards and bulletins are readable, cars don't block entrances, lighting isn't dim, the loop system works, heating systems are effective, access to a toilet is straightforward, instructions to stand, sit or kneel aren't onerous and so on. It may also be important to review terminology that emphasizes 'young families' at the expense of older, single people.

Remember that older people have probably known suffering and got through it Suffering is new territory for younger people but older generations have known what it is to be worked to exhaustion or to follow a dream and find it's a nightmare. They've known death and disaster in different forms and somehow they've come through the fire. They've been sensitized to what suffering does to a person and to their faith, and they may have a tale to tell and time to listen.

Older age can be a time to return to church The quiet voice that cried out from somewhere deep within, but was drowned out by the speed and fury of life, may now come to be heard more clearly, asking deeper questions about meaning, purpose and fulfilment. A strange yearning to make contact with 'something more' may surface and ministers should be alert to those bigger questions that lie there, looking for exploration and not be distracted by that odd ministerial conviction that they should be jolly and superficial.

Older people can be great pray-ers If you want something to be prayed about, go to the wise old saints.

Quick idea: memory boxes

Memory boxes can give great enjoyment. A group of older people can be invited to find a box, perhaps the size of a shoebox, and to start filling it with objects with special meaning and sentimental value. These will usually say something significant about the person's life story, relationships, values, faith and more. A memory box might contain the ticket for a Beatles concert or a badge from work, the invitation to a wedding or a lock of a loved one's hair, a photo from a special holiday or pebbles from a favourite beach. It may contain a CD, a recipe, a letter, a diary, a cross and perhaps something to hold. A group session can consist of each member talking about two or three objects from their box – what they are and why they're there. The box should be decorated, the contents loved and the objects explained in a note. The box is for future generations, but also for the present as they help the person work out something of 'who I am and what's important to me.' This idea can transfer to many different settings.

Ministry with older people

We do well to realize that in our work with older people, we might be rehearsing our own future. In what ways can we enjoy the participation of older people in the life of the Church?

- *Wisdom for committees and working groups* This is where we need to recognize the life experience and particular gifts of older people who have 'been there' and taken the knocks, seen success and failure, and experienced some of the pitfalls and possibilities. Such contributors need not be of the 'been there, done that, no good' variety, but genuine encouragers of new projects and programmes.
- *Lunch clubs* which take the Saga definition of 50+ as the usual criterion of membership. Such lunches shouldn't compromise on quality. They should also use the gifts and skills of members, so that it doesn't seem as if Lady Bountiful is 'doing good' again. As well as the meal and friendship, members can be interviewed about their lives or variations of *Desert Island Discs* can be used to tell their story. Invited guests could speak; they could play games and schoolchildren could be involved. The possibilities are plentiful.
- *Appropriate variations in styles of worship* Many churches offer midweek morning Communion with a considerable following. Some have as many as fifty regulars, making it another main congregation in the life of the church. It can be followed by good coffee, Bible study or discussion, a light lunch and local shopping – in any permutation. This midweek spot serves many older people well as it focuses on their age group and offers age-appropriate activities, rather more than the Sunday morning jamboree. Other forms of worship that may be useful can be 'Songs of Praise', using popular chosen hymns and preceded or followed by a good tea. Café church on a Sunday afternoon can allow engagement with speakers on important faith issues in an extended, informal setting. Contemplative

services with prayer stations can offer a spacious opportunity for reflection and prayer that other services don't.

- *Pairing up of any-age car drivers with older, less mobile people for transport* to church or for shopping, prescriptions, hospital appointments and so on. The car drivers might themselves be older people and, hopefully, friendships are formed. We always need to be aware of safeguarding issues in setting up such schemes because they might involve vulnerable adults.

- *Involvement in ministry* Older people may be involved in leading worship, singing in the choir, bell-ringing, children's work, homegroup leadership, church finance, pastoral visiting, ministry with asylum seekers, food banks, homeless people's support, Church Action on Poverty, Christian Aid Week collections and so on. But they might also want to get involved with Open the Book in schools, Messy Church, mentoring, listening to reading in school and more. Time, readiness and ability are the determinants of these activities, not age.

- *Holiday weeks for older people* These parallel the well-established holiday weeks for children. A summer week can be planned to involve talks, music, films, outings and 'eatings', and can easily include craft afternoons where the creative potential that's in each one of us can be released through paint, clay, collage, poetry, card-making, jewellery and more.

- *Practical jobs* I know a church where a group of older people with practical skills have set themselves up as the 'Happy Bodgers', volunteering to take on small practical jobs around the homes of parishioners. These are the jobs that fall annoyingly beyond the everyday skills of a householder, but short of the need for a professional. In some contexts this service could include helping with a computer or filling in complicated forms. Safeguarding issues are again relevant.

- *Life-story work* Memory boxes have already been mentioned. A more linear approach to drawing the different threads of life together is life-story work that helps people, one to one, tell of key incidents, reflect on significant relationships, recall major turning points and thereby get a sense of their life's work and worth. Conversation can lead to audio or video recording, creating a scrapbook or, indeed, writing a full or partial narrative. While in his eighties, my father-in-law wrote over a hundred pages on his long life, which gave our family fascinating insights, including into his time on the Arctic convoys and at D-Day. It also gave him some sense, I believe, of completion: 'This is what I achieved, what I made of life, what I enjoyed.' This life-story work can also be done intergenerationally and enable young people to appreciate the richness of the lives they might otherwise have seen as simply 'past it'.

- *Dementia-friendly churches* There are many ways in which a church can become dementia-friendly. A coordinator can be appointed to oversee opportunities. A four-session course with the organization Dementia Friendly Churches could be followed (see 'Resources' below). Groups that welcome people living with dementia often use singing as a lovely way to engage memories and encourage participation. Worship services can also be adapted in small ways to be more helpful to those living with dementia.

- *The Internet and social media* Many older people are very adept at new communication technologies. This can form the basis of blogs, online communities and assistance offered to the Church and other individuals. Churches are always looking for someone to run their websites.

- *Waiting for the last bus* This evocative title of a book by Richard Holloway raises the inevitable issue of how churches can help older people approach the inevitability of dying. Death Cafés have already been mentioned (see **Death**) as a context where death and dying can be discussed with a light touch. There are excellent courses (see 'Resources' below) where customized or ongoing groups can try various sessions. People can be encouraged to plan their funeral with the readings, poetry, hymns, music and the style of the service worked out – hopefully well in advance. Done in a group, this can be a focus for reminiscence and spiritual stories. This activity can include thinking out and writing down what people would like to receive by way of spiritual support – visits, yes, but what about Communion, anointing, prayers and so on? An 'Advent sermon course' on the meaning of resurrection might be useful, with Bible study material alongside. What about a link on the church website to key organizations relevant to death and bereavement? A 'Bereavement Support Group' can be a lifeline.

Tailpiece: some facts for those who like this sort of thing

- People aged 50 or over will make up over half the adult population of the UK in fewer than 20 years.
- In the UK, there are now more people over 60 than under 18.
- The over-65s will make up one-third of the population of developed countries by 2050.
- In 30 years' time, in the UK, the number of over-75s will have doubled.
- Up to 3.8 million older people in the UK live alone, 70 per cent of whom are women.
- More than 850,000 people are living with dementia, and the number is set to be 2 million by 2050.[1]

Resources

Alzheimer's Society (<www.alzheimers.org.uk>).

The Anna Chaplaincy: Offering spiritual care in later life, (<www.annachaplaincy.org.uk/>)

The Church of England, 'Funerals' (including 'Grave Talk')(<www.churchofenglandfunerals.org>).

Dementia Action Alliance (<www.nationaldementiaaction.org.uk>).

Dementia Friendly Churches (<www.dementiafriendlychurch.org.uk>).

Dementia UK (<www.dementiauk.org>).

O Older people

Diocese of Oxford, 'Spiritual Care for Older People' (SCOP), (<www.oxford.anglican.org/mission-ministry/making-a-difference/ageing>). A wealth of online material, including the valuable factsheet 'The extra dimension' and *Living Well in the End Times*.

K. Albans and M. Johnson, *God, Me and Being Very Old: Stories of spirituality in later life*, (London: SCM Press, 2013).

Richard Holloway, *Waiting for the Last Bus* (Edinburgh: Canongate, 2018).

The Methodist Church and the Church of England, *Seasons of My Soul: Conversations in the second half of life* (London: Methodist Publishing House, 2014).

Sue Pickering, *Creative Ideas for Ministry with the Aged: Liturgies, prayers and resources* (Norwich: Canterbury Press, 2014).

David Winter, *At the End of the Day: Living well in the departure lounge* (Abingdon: BRF, 2013).

Tom Wright, *Surprised by Hope: Original, provocative and practical* (London: SPCK, 2011).

P

Prayer

The most important thing we do in ministry is pray. Everything we do in ministry is an overflow of the love of God in our lives, so if we're running on empty there won't be much to share; we might keep turning the handle but all the vigour will have gone out of our ministry, which ends up powerless and graceless. If prayer is so fundamental to living faithfully, it also follows that one of our most important tasks is to help others to pray, in the ways that suit them best.

Starters

Here are some basics to offer as we learn together about praying (we're all serial beginners at prayer).

- *Prayer is natural to nearly all men and women* It starts with the most common of instincts – gratitude, wonder, regret and need. We all know what those feel like. Prayer is when we take those instincts and stretch them out intentionally in the direction of God. Then gratitude becomes thanksgiving, wonder becomes adoration, regret becomes confession, and responding to need becomes intercession.
- Behind that stretching out of our natural instincts there lies an even simpler image. *Prayer is like sunbathing; we go out to sunbathe in the love of God* We can't turn up the heat of the

sun any higher; we can only choose to lie in it or not. There may be clouds in the way at times (stuff happens) but the love of God for us is constant; we can't make God love us more, nor can we make him love us less. If we change the image slightly, St John of the Cross says helpfully, 'The sun is up early and ready to shine in – if you open the curtains.' Prayer, then, is opening the curtains.

- Let's change the image again. St Augustine said that *prayer is taking a chalice to the fountain to be filled.* God's grace is constantly bubbling up throughout life and we go to this fountain to catch the overflow. We then go and share God's grace with others throughout the day.

- *Prayer is taking our concerns from the head to the heart* We're constantly thinking, analysing and taking in information, and we carry all those thoughts and concerns in our minds. Prayer eases the log jam, taking those concerns for others and for ourselves to the warmer embrace of the heart, where God is always at work.

- *We learn to pray by praying* We start simply by turning up. Soldiers in the First World War sang, 'We're here because we're here because we're here because we're here.' Until we're 'here' we can't encounter God. It's obvious really. So let's pray.

- *There are no right or wrong ways to pray* We need to be assured that our own way of praying will be as unique as our fingerprints. We may learn ways of prayer that many before us have found to be helpful, but no esoteric techniques are required and there are no exams.

- *Intercession is important as part of a larger fabric of prayer* Intercession is the best way we have of loving someone, although we need to beware of dangerous expectations. J.John wisely says that we pray not to *move* the hand of God but to *hold* the hand of God. Overly interventionist understandings of prayer can sometimes be spiritually damaging, leading to failure, guilt and the weakening of faith. It might help to speak of God working more from the 'inside out' than the 'outside in,' but always working flat out, pressing nature to its furthest reaches where the usual may become the unusual – something we then call a miracle. Answers to prayer are ultimately mysterious because they rest in God, not in our own functional view of reality. Intercession, then, is a central concern of prayer but there's more to engage in – thanksgiving, confession, meditation and silence being just some.

- *Prayer isn't a technique; it's a relationship* Relationships are lived out in a multitude of ways – joyfully, gratefully, painfully, with love, curiosity, ecstasy, regret and so much more. Sometimes relationships can even be boring. St Teresa of Avila was known sometimes to shake her hourglass during prayer because she was so impatient and bored. If it was good enough for her . . .

Prayer as a relationship

When teaching about prayer, I've found it helpful to use the following image, stating the obvious that our most important relationships tend to have many different dimensions.

'Just getting on with it'

I don't obsess all the time about the fact that I'm married. I accept that relationship as the bedrock of my life and just get on with living the day, perhaps occasionally remembering my wife happily or prayerfully, depending on what her day holds. So it is with prayer; we don't need to be overly pious, we simply know that we are 'in Christ' and get on with living, occasionally 'practising the presence of God'.

Chatting

When we're with good friends for the day, we chat easily about ordinary things. There's nothing forced or awkward about chatting; it just flows. So it is with prayer. We can chat with God at any time about anything – the task we're involved in, the ambulance or police siren signalling some crisis, the news item that challenges or moves us, the friend who's just shared a problem with us. But chatting isn't just saying 'arrow prayers'. Chatting can mean holding a hand cross, praying as we walk the dog, punctuating the day with moments of quiet recollection, praying the Jesus Prayer ('Lord Jesus Christ, Son of God, have mercy on me, a sinner.') It's natural.

Talking
This is more deliberate than chatting. In our close relationships, it's when we give ourselves to the other person and spend time listening, exchanging thoughts, learning about the other. In prayer, this is the special time with God, without which our relationship won't deepen. We might use:

- Bible notes followed by prayer. Scripture opens the heart;
- a daily office such as 'Common Worship' or 'Celtic Daily Prayer' – structure creates freedom;
- a pneumonic such as PRAY (Prepare, Remember the good in thankfulness and the bad in confession, Ask for others, You – your own needs this day);
- online resources such as the Jesuit *Sacred Space*.

There's so much more to say about all this; it's embarrassing to be so brief!

Intimacy
Our closest relationships don't need so many words; we have a level of understanding that means that silence, touch, a look and so on are not only sufficient but preferable. Words can get in the way of our deepest affections. So it is with prayer. As the journey

goes on, many people find that words are less necessary and they explore lectio divina for deeper Bible reading, Ignatian meditation to explore the gospel through the senses, the Examen for daily awareness of God's presence and centring prayer in order to lay themselves open to God. Praying through both the natural world and through the arts (paintings, poetry, music) offer other rich resources for prayer, without which many of us would dry out spiritually. All these ways of praying can bring us into an intimate encounter with God. They're not about a *transaction with* God, they're about *transformation by* God.

Prayer for extroverts
So much teaching about prayer frustrates extroverts because it emphasizes the quiet inner journey, whereas they get their energy and renewal from engaging with the outer world. An extrovert might well respond best to:

- prayer in public worship;
- prayer of a more meditative kind such as Taizé or a quiet service with prayer stations;
- prayer groups, sharing the experience of prayer and learning from others;
- praying while outdoors, walking to the shops, jogging, cycling or walking the dog;
- praying with a friend or two in a regular, committed way;
- praying while working on something else;
- prayer as loving action.

Having said that, many extroverts find they also need the quiet experience of prayer to 'round out' their personality type and gain a greater integration and wholeness (Jung called it individuation). You find many extroverts at silent retreats and quiet days.

Quick idea: a Festival of Prayer

This is a day, a weekend or even a week in which the focus is on different ways to pray. Let's take a weekend. This could start on the Friday evening with a *speaker from the wider church or a forum* in which local Christians are invited to speak honestly of their own prayer journey. The venue for the weekend could be a combination of church, hall, school or other places, and the main space could be set out with *prayer stations* for use throughout the weekend. The whole of Saturday or Saturday morning could be a *Quiet Day*, a structured time but with plenty of space to use the prayer stations and other resources. Saturday afternoon could be spent on a *Prayer Walk*. Late afternoon or evening of the Saturday could be used for watching a *film* or TV series that raises issues about the spiritual journey (*The Way* about the journey to Santiago de Compostela; *Of Gods and Men* about the martyrdom of seven monks in Algeria; *Broken* about a priest facing personal and ministerial challenges in urban Britain; *The Monastery* about monastic life in England today). *Sunday morning worship* would focus on prayer and the prayer stations would be available all day. *Sunday evening worship* could depend on the tradition – a praise service or choral evensong.

Encouraging prayer in ministry

If it is indeed the case that one of our main tasks in lay and ordained ministry is to help people to pray, we need to think carefully about the best means of doing that in our own particular situation. Every context and every group will need something different. Here are ten ideas:

1 The prayer group

It's always worth asking if there is a group of people who would simply like to pray for the life of the church and in doing so to learn more about prayer. Then you can share and pray about different issues in sequence (the past week, strategy and growth, special concerns and upcoming events). Such a group can be the fire at the heart of church life.

2 Short courses of prayer
This could consist of four sessions exploring 'Christ in Quiet' or looking at different spiritual traditions (Benedictine, Ignatian, Celtic, Franciscan) or methods of prayer (such as the Examen, the Jesus Prayer, Centring prayer).

3 Sermon course
When did you last hear a sermon on prayer – and not just with a vague exhortation to 'pray more' or 'pray harder'? Examine Jesus' practice of prayer; it's clear his life was saturated in prayer. A sermon course could be deeply rooted in Scripture, traditions of prayer and personal experience.

4 Intercessions workshops
This could take the form of a half day helping those who lead intercessions in services to think through and improve their style of doing so. The way intercessions are led can not only enrich worship but can help people learn more about how they can pray themselves (see 'Resources' below).

Contemplative prayer services
Many Christians who have been on the road for some time long for quieter forms of worship where there's space to pray in different ways, to ponder, linger, wonder and rest. One of the best ways of offering time for this is to use prayer stations around the church with imaginative and spacious ways to pray at each point. People can wander around in their own time, perhaps in subdued light with quiet music and incense creating a helpful atmosphere for prayer. There are websites full of ideas for these

prayer stations (see 'Resources' below). At the end, a gentle service of Night Prayer can round things off.

Quiet days
A group could go away to a retreat centre or a generous person's large house and have a quiet day with two or three short inputs: worship at the start and finish, a wide variety of books and art materials, hopefully a garden, maybe a music room with CDs and more, all of which people can use in their own time. Such a restful day is usually deeply valued.

Retreat in daily life
Many Anglican dioceses have small groups of people who will come to a church each night for a week and meet those who want to deepen their prayer life, one to one. This regular meeting for people to talk over their current experience and be offered other ways of praying, can be transformative. The difficulty lies in persuading people that this won't be terrifying! It won't, but keep reassuring and encouraging.

Pilgrimage
Travelling together to a place of pilgrimage can give a great boost to prayer. Places can range from a local cathedral to the Holy Land, taking in places such as Iona, Lindisfarne, Canterbury, Durham, Walsingham, Rome, Assisi and scores of other places. A rhythm of daily prayer can be established, resources are offered and the result can be that prayer associated with a particular place comes alive and spills over into an enthusiasm for more encounters with God.

Books and websites
Of the writing of books on prayer there is no end, but the right book offered at the right time can be life changing. The skill in our ministry lies in discerning which book or website it is.

Example

The way we pray with people, either in public or personal prayer, can be hugely influential. We have to be true to ourselves, but it can be helpful if we are brief (so we don't scare people with long perorations), honest (so we show that anything is acceptable), natural (so we demonstrate that 'um-er' is fine too) and imaginative (so we widen horizons on prayer).

> **Tailpiece: wading in the water**
>
> A great and mighty river flows throughout history toward the healing and restoration of all things. You know how the story ends: love conquers death, a new heaven and earth are established, and the God of love and justice puts things to rights. Our Creator is carrying every corner of creation into a beautiful future. Jesus Christ referred to this river as the kingdom of God, a realm where the things that God wants to happen, happen . . . You and I have been invited to swim with this eternal current for the sake of the world. Jesus didn't merely invite us to believe about the river . . . The invitation is to wade into the river and swim . . . Yet so many of us miss the invitation. We concentrate on perfecting our beliefs but never step into the water . . . I missed the invitation for years. I believed Christian ideas, prayed Christian prayers and attended Christian events, but I never learned to swim with Christ in the river of God . . . Grace alone makes the river flow, *but we need to wade into the water*.[1]

Resources

There are, of course, vast numbers of books on prayer, so I'm not choosing the older classics, but simply some more recent, widely read books.

Stephen Cottrell, *How to Pray: Alone, with others, at any time, in any place* (London: Church House Publishing, 2010).

Richard Foster, *Celebration of Discipline: The path to spiritual growth* (London: Hodder & Stoughton, revised 1989).

Pete Greig, *How to Pray: A simple guide for normal people* (London: Hodder & Stoughton, 2019).

IgnatianSpirituality.com for a very short course on prayer, with further links (available at: <www.ignatianspirituality.com>).

Aaron Niequist, *The Eternal Current: How a practice-based faith can save us from drowning* (New York: Waterbrook, 2018).

Pinterest for prayer stations (<www.pinterest.co.uk/jlhart76/prayer-stations/>).

John Pritchard, *How to Pray: A practical handbook* (London: SPCK, reissued 2011).

John Pritchard, *The Intercessions Handbook/The Second Intercessions Handbook/ The Intercessions Resource Book* (London: SPCK, 1997, 2004, 2014).

Ronald Rolheiser, *Sacred Fire: A vision for a deeper human and Christian maturity* (New York: Image, 2014).

Bonnie Thurston, *For God Alone: A primer on prayer* (London: Darton, Longman & Todd, 2009).

24-7 Prayer, The Prayer Course (based on Pete Greig's book above)(available at: <www.prayercourse.org>).

Apps

The Church of England, *Daily Prayer, Reflections for Daily Prayer, Time to Pray* available from the App Store under 'Daily Prayer'.

P

Preaching

This chapter is mostly relevant to those who find themselves entrusted with the privilege of preaching in church. However, it may also be of value to others who have to give Christian talks in other contexts or to those who are interested in the whole process of preaching. All ordained ministers and many lay ministers preach. It may not be our particular gift but still we do it; it goes with the job. We have to do our very best, for God and for God's people.

The Times reported a few years ago on a church in Jacksonville, Florida, that, until the previous week, had been led by the Revd Melvyn Nurse. Trying to illustrate his sermon about the temptations of sin, he fumbled in his cassock pocket and produced a .357-caliber Magnum. He inserted a blank, spun the cylinder, put the gun to his temple and, after each sin, pulled the trigger to show how easy it was to fall into temptation. Unfortunately, on his third sin, the 'blank' went off, killing him.[1]

Such extreme measures to enliven our preaching are unnecessary! Nevertheless, we all need to keep working on our preaching, improving content, style and delivery. The massive success of TED talks shows that there's still a hunger for well-presented material on subjects of value. It's worth reflecting on the three core components of these talks, according to public speaking coach Carmine Gallo.[2] TED talks are *emotional* in that they touch the heart, *novel* in that they offer new information or a new approach and *memorable* in that they stay with the listener and aren't erased after a few minutes. How does our last sermon stand up to that analysis?

A congregation often leaves church humming a hymn tune. How often do people leave church humming the sermon?

What is preaching?

At its simplest, preaching is a set of words (a sermon) about the word (Scripture) about the Word (Jesus). My pulpit prayer is: 'May these spoken words be faithful to the written word and lead us to the living Word, Jesus Christ our Lord.'

The *spoken words* need to be carefully chosen, tested for precision and crafted with love. We live in a society that's increasingly careless and indiscriminate with words. In a culture of 'fake news' and plain lying, respect for truth is at a premium. In our preaching, we have a responsibility to use words that are full of grace and truth, because they point to the One who was himself full of those qualities.

There's a more searching question for preachers: will we determine not to declare as truth things that we haven't really thought about ourselves? It's comparatively easy to trot out second-hand ideas that haven't been through the mill of our own hard thinking. Integrity demands we've tested what we're talking about.

The *written word* is our basic raw material, what's been called 'food for wrestlers'. We wrestle with Scripture and, like Jacob, expect to go away limping but inspired. What the congregation wants, however, is not to hear how clever the preacher is and how many commentaries he or she has devoured, but how what was written *then* in a particular context speaks *now* in ours. People, by and large, don't come to church desperately anxious to discover what happened to the Jebusites. Rather, what does their story say to ours? Nor is it our job to judge Scripture from our superior position atop the dung heap of twenty-first century conventional wisdom; rather we put ourselves under the authority of Scripture, even as we use our informed intelligence to understand and interpret it.

We pray that these *spoken words* will be faithful to the *written word*, but only so that they may lead us to the *living Word* who is Jesus Christ himself. A theological college student went to his tutor with a copy of a sermon he was going to preach. 'Will it do?' he asked. 'Will it do *what*?' said the tutor. What will our sermons do? It's important to know what we want to come out of the sermon for the listener. What is the sermon for? What do we expect to happen? Whatever else we say in answer to those questions, we need to be praying that our preaching will in some way lead people to Christ. That's the acid test. Does the litmus paper change colour because people are encountering the living God?

The essentials

Daring to write about preaching is a bit like writing about being Christlike – who on earth am I to tell anyone else how to do it? There are as many different ways to preach as there are preachers, because preaching has to involve the personality of the preacher. All I offer, therefore, are some principles that I believe are essential to all of us, however we work them out.

- *Speak to a context* A Cambridge academic once began a sermon in a service for college servants: 'The ontological argument for the existence of God has in recent years, largely under Teutonic influence, been relegated to a position of comparative inferiority in the armoury of Christian apologetics.' Not a winning start. We have to know our congregation, their interests, concerns, preoccupations and so on. Otherwise we preach in a vacuum.
- *Soak yourself in the text* We have to pan the gold out of it, but we must avoid telling the congregation everything we know.

It's the distilling of knowledge that's the art. The key move in our sermon preparation is to listen for the sting in the biblical passage. Where does it hit home? Where does it collide with our comfortable values? Where does it subvert the usual scripts that our culture works from? Where does it re-describe the world more truthfully? The sting is where we begin to work in sermon preparation.

- *Distil a single rich idea* We need to think not of the message but the *idea* behind the message. Think of the plethora of television adverts for cars. They don't give us any particular message about the car's performance; they give us an image, an idea, that this car is the one that will express and embody who we are or want to be. They're selling an idea. Jesus preached in idea form: 'The kingdom of heaven,' he said, 'is like a mustard seed.' Finding this idea and being able to articulate it in a single sentence is the most exacting but most fruitful part of sermon preparation and, until we've found it, we shouldn't proceed.

- *Use stories whenever possible* We live in a culture soaked in stories. It seems that every conversation, video on YouTube, series on Netflix, article in the paper, advert on television, film, novel and stand-up routine depends on telling a story. Jesus did it all the time. 'There was a man who had two sons . . .' 'A man was going down from Jerusalem to Jericho . . .' 'Suppose one of you has a friend and you go to him at midnight . . .' His characteristic teaching style was through parables that he tossed seemingly carelessly into his hearers' hearts to subvert old, worn-out ways of thinking. So today, watch how any human group perks up when the speaker tells a story. Stories aren't nice bits of padding to fill out a sermon; they're the way we all communicate in daily life and the way to communicate the grace and truth of Jesus in our preaching and teaching. Stories live on, while concepts fade quickly away (see **Narrative**).

- *Enrich your language* (if you'll pardon the expression). Bland language speaks of a bland faith, whereas a palette of words that bring colour and life to what we're saying is much more fun. Why say 'Jesus entered the Temple' when you could say 'Jesus stormed into the Temple . . .'? Why say 'I was waiting at the bus-stop' when you could say 'I was past impatient, stamping my feet and muttering darkly about inefficient bus companies . . .'? Why say 'Jesus was sitting by the well' when you could say, 'He was dog-tired. The heat was blistering and the water was twenty feet down the well . . .'? There's joy in heaven over one boring word that's replaced by a more vivid one.

- *Don't be afraid of humour* Attempts at humour when the preacher can't deliver a punchline or a particularly old joke staggers out of the sermon, fatally wounded, are experiences that may have put many ministers off ever using humour in their preaching. But humour is part of our humanity. How many other animals laugh? Humour lightens our days and delivers truth with subtle effectiveness. It should be used carefully but without fear. If heaven is a place without jokes, wit and hyperbole, it will be a very boring existence. I'm sure I sometimes catch the odd rumble of laughter overflowing heaven's gates; Peter must be doing his stand-up again . . .

- *Find your voice* No one else will preach as we do, nor should we try and be someone else in our style of preaching. We have to find what works and feels comfortable to us, while always being open to alter and improve. Not everyone will appreciate our style of course; that's not because it's an evil and adulterous generation, it's simply because they're different too. The one thing it's good to keep an eye on, however, is how the congregation use their watches – if they're shaking them to see if they're broken, we've probably gone on too long.

- *Don't always preach the same sermon* As the old saying goes, 'Ten thousand thousand are their texts, but all their sermons one.'

Quick idea: feedback

It's very valuable to set up a regular or occasional form of feedback for our preaching. All ministers are vulnerable after preaching but a trusted person or two who give constructive feedback soon after the sermon are certainly worth a box of chocolates or a bottle of wine. How did it come across? Was it clear, helpful, challenging and inspiring? Was my delivery alive or wooden? Did I swallow the ends of my sentences? How effective were the stories? Did it start and end strongly? Did you agree? Did you stay awake? The feedback can be given briefly over coffee after the service, by meeting the next day or even by filling in a simple feedback sheet if you're that kind of hyper-organized person. People are often flattered and feel privileged to be asked to help in this way and will gladly give the time. Warning: your spouse may get fed up of being the one who has to say nice things because they live with you . . .

Sermon structure

When faced with a blank sheet or a blank mind, having a possible structure to work with can be reassuring. Again, I hesitate to give advice when ministers are so different in style, but the following has been a general template I've found useful, adapted from the book *Communicating for a Change*.[3]

Me: Make an immediate connection with the congregation by telling a personal story that introduces the 'idea' (see 'The essentials' above) that the sermon is going to explore.

Us: Widen out the issue from your personal story to the common experience of many listeners. This identifies the tension that needs examining and puts it in the wider context of our puzzles and struggles in life. It's why this sermon is being preached.

God: This is where the gospel comes in, giving divine wisdom that offers a way of resolving the tension. The good news here mustn't be in abstract form. What has been opened out in human shape needs to be met in the embodied language of Jesus: we mustn't slip into the language of Zion. Nor must we slip into law when the gospel is about grace. That's a vital question to ask ourselves every time: is this sermon going to come across as law or grace?

Us: How might this new understanding of the issue be worked out in practice? This is the application part of the sermon. The gospel 'idea' is now clearly revealed for all to see, so how does it work? Again, we must be concrete. A shower of examples or a particularly strong story may work best.

God and us: This brings the sermon home with both challenge and inspiration, tying together both God's invitation and our response. Using the image of flight, sermons need a strong, clear landing and it has to be said that many sermons stay aloft long after the flight is over. We need to know how to land.

A variation on this structure is found in Lowry's seminal book *The Homiletical Plot*.[4] He describes five slightly different stages in this way.

1 Upset the equilibrium.
2 Analyse the discrepancy.
3 Disclose the clue to the resolution.
4 Experience the gospel.
5 Anticipate the consequences.

(Or, in human terms: oops, hmm, aha, wow, yeah!)

Tailpiece: words of encouragement

Thomas Carlyle said: 'Who, having been called to be a preacher, would stoop to be a king?'

A friend met the sceptical philosopher David Hume hurrying down the road. 'Can't stop,' said the great man, 'I'm off to hear George Whitfield preach.' 'But you don't believe a word of it,' replied his astonished friend. 'No, but Whitfield does,' said David Hume.

John Donne was Dean of St Paul's. He was preaching outdoors and had gone on for two hours. As he came to a stop, the crowd shouted, 'More, more.' (That's never been my experience, but may it be yours.)

Martin Luther wrote (without regard to today's inclusive language):

A good preacher should have these properties and virtues: first, he should be able to teach in a right and orderly way. Second, he should have a good wit. Third, he should be able to speak well. Fourth, he should have a good voice. Fifth, a good memory. Sixth, he should know when to stop. Seventh, he should make sure of his material and be diligent. Eighth, he should stake body and blood, goods and honour on it. Ninth, he must suffer himself to be vexed and flayed by everyone.

Encouraged?

Resources

Barbara Brown Taylor, *The Preaching Life: Living out your vocation* (London: Canterbury Press, 2013).

Kate Bruce and Jamie Harrison, *Wrestling with the Word: Preaching on tricky texts* (London: SPCK, 2016).

The College of Preachers, *The Preacher*, quarterly magazine (available online at: <www.collegeofpreachers.co.uk>).

Church Times, Festival of Preaching (<www.churchtimes.co.uk>).

David Day, *A Preaching Workbook* (London: SPCK, 1998).

David Day, *Embodying the Word: A preacher's guide* (London: SPCK, 2005).

David Day, Jeff Astley and Lesley J. Francis (eds), *A Reader on Preaching; Making connections* (Aldershot: Ashgate, 2005).

Andy Stanley and Lane Jones, *Communicating for a Change: Seven keys to irresistable communication* (Colorado Springs, CO: Multnomah, 2006).

Simon Vibert, *Excellence in Preaching* (Nottingham: IVP, 2011).

Q
Questions

We rarely ask the kind of questions our forefathers asked, like 'How is it with your soul?' Yet questions are a key tool in ministry. More widely, there are three overlapping areas in which questions are significant.

1 The use of questions in various forms of ministry.
2 The questioning of faith in a sceptical culture.
3 Our own questioning of faith in times of difficulty.

The use of questions in ministry

Jesus asked a lot of questions. It was part of the Jewish tradition of Midrash that asked questions of ancient texts – questions that were sometimes answered and sometimes left open. Jesus used questions to open up people's thinking about the Law, about themselves and about how they related to God.

Think of some of the familiar questions Jesus asked in the Gospels. 'What do you want me to do for you?' asked of a blind man by the roadside. 'Has no one condemned you?' asked of a woman dangerously caught in the act of adultery. 'Which of these was a neighbour to the man who fell among thieves?' asked of a lawyer trying to test him. 'Who do you say that I am?' asked of the disciples away on retreat in Caesarea Philippi. 'Why are you weeping?' asked of Mary Magdalene in the garden. 'What things?' asked of two despondent disciples walking to Emmaus. And so on.

Once you start noticing them, Jesus' questions are all over the Gospels. They enabled Jesus to listen. They showed respect. They showed he wasn't making assumptions.

Questions are like that. They hold a situation open; they don't close it down to stock answers and routine interpretations. They give space. They encourage curiosity and discovery. They keep you thinking.

Many of us will be familiar with so-called 'conversations' that consist of alternate statements made from behind walls of self-interest, with no attempt to engage with what the other has said. The result is an exchange of anecdote, opinion or prejudice, but no real encounter. Jesus wanted honest engagement with people, so he asked questions.

The right question at the right time can be transformative. But questions are also basic tools of interaction. I'm sometimes amazed at an ordained minister, perhaps at a conference, sitting in silence at a meal with someone they don't know, and apparently unable or unwilling to communicate with that person. Or I'm saddened to hear of a minister who parishioners say doesn't know how to engage with them. A few questions will open up a world of issues. Just ask people about themselves – it's so simple.

When the conversation has a more significant purpose, again the right question can quickly move things on. 'How's life?' we ask. 'Not bad,' they say. 'Only not bad? What's going on then?' Or, 'So what are your headlines at the moment?' When I wanted to cut to the chase with some parishioners I would ask, playfully but seriously, 'So how's God then?' Or, 'What's saving your life at present?' And we were off . . .

Ministry brings us into contact with decision-makers of all sorts, from local councillors to headteachers, from business leaders to charity workers. Again, the right question can open up deep conversations. 'What gets you out of bed in the morning?' 'What's the biggest question you're having to ask yourself at present?' 'What would make the most significant difference to the problems you face?' 'What could the church offer?'

We have to be careful to distinguish between helpful questions and interrogation. A friend once took me to task for making him feel a bit like an onion being peeled back one layer after another. Healthy questions should feel like a gift, not an inquisition.

Questions are some of our most valuable tools in ministry. Jesus knew it and so must we.

The questioning of faith in a secular culture

Christian faith is fair game in our culture. So is any religious belief. But instead of getting into immediate defensive/aggressive mode, we would do well to consider again why unbelief is reasonable to so many and to consider, more generally, the value of questions. There are no knock-down proofs for the existence of God and there's a good deal stacked against it – the prevalence of personal suffering and physical disaster, for example, or the poor performance of Christians down the centuries. Singer Labi Siffre once wrote, 'The only religions worthy of respect are those with the following essential text: "Brothers and sisters, believe me when I say we have, at least, a fifty-fifty chance of being wrong." Now, let us pray.' Faith is the best gamble we ever make – so let's live and pray on that basis, but not ridicule unbelief.

Instead of being defensive in the face of scepticism we should be prepared to join in the honest exploration of questions of truth. Thomas Aquinas maintained that God is not the answer; God is the question. Goethe too suggested that, 'The conflict of faith and scepticism remains the proper, the only, the deepest theme of the history of the world and of mankind.'[1]

The proper mode for us to engage with people's religious questions is one of conversation, exploration, curiosity, suggestion, invitation and so on. It's quite possible to be tentative and positive at the same time. To say, 'I wonder if . . .' suits our age much better than noisy statements, honey-coated accusations ('With all due respect . . .') and unconvincing bluster. It's the tone that matters. I remember to my shame when officiating at weddings, accusingly holding the eye of men (it was usually men) who weren't singing, as if to shame them into song. They may well not have believed any of it, but equally they might simply have been sure they couldn't sing and so didn't. Now at services where there are probably a large number of doubters or non-believers, I will sometimes say before the creed, 'To the extent that you feel comfortable, please join in the classic words of Christian belief.' The tone isn't accusatory but permissive and wins more of a hearing in the long run.

Maybe the Church doesn't ask enough first-order questions, preferring to discuss, if not the number of angels you can fit on a pinhead, at least the niceties of canon-law revision or which memorials are appropriate in a churchyard. The big questions are what people are interested in: about God, human nature, suffering, prayer, the earth. Rowan Williams wrote, 'Churches and other faith groups might be called trustees or custodians of the long-term questions because they own a vision of human nature that does not depend on political fashions and majorities.'[2]

In a parish I served in Taunton, we had a group called 'No Holds Barred' where any question could be asked. It was for those clinging on to faith or wondering about it. The premise was that there were no right or wrong answers and the vicar wouldn't come in with 'the right answer' at the end. Discussion topics were chosen by the group and led by the members. As I mentioned under **Evangelism**, in a parish I served, the atmosphere was relaxed, helped by the roaring fire, good coffee and whisky following. It was an open, accepting forum for exploration and caught the mood for many.

It's the same with groups of enquirers meeting in coffee shops or the discussion at many of the events known (anachronistically) as 'men's breakfasts'. We're not here to bludgeon anyone with The-Truth-As-We-Know-It but to engage positively with the real questions people have. If we're confident in the truth of the gospel, we'll believe that if we pursue the truth far enough, we'll bump into Jesus Christ, who is himself the Truth.

Quick idea: an hour for God

One of the most important things we do in ministry is to talk with people about their deepest feelings to do with faith. Sadly, we often find ourselves talking about the things of faith rather than faith itself – about church instead of God. So we might take a period of time, say Lent, and offer an hour to anyone who wants to talk about their spiritual journey. The offer could be to talk with one of a number of people if there's a ministry team. Our first and major task is to listen very carefully and discern what's really being said – the bass line rather than the more obvious melody. We can use several questions, such as:

- what would you like to talk about?
- where did your faith journey start?
- what have been the main changes in your faith since the early days?
- what do you do when you pray?
- what would you like to understand better?
- what's going to church like for you?
- what aspect of faith do you find most rewarding and which is most hard work?

It might be helpful to give those example questions to the person beforehand. During the conversation we keep listening, reflect back what we hear, make suggestions, share parts of our own story and offer resources. At the end of the conversation we can ask what the other person will take away from it and, if it feels appropriate, we could suggest a spiritual accompanier. Take note, the conversation must be encouraging, confidential and not judgemental.

Our own questioning of faith

Then there are our own questions to face. Not the doubts that pass through our minds when we wonder if anyone is really awake during our sermon, but the black crow of doubt that flaps across the night sky and sends a frisson of fear slicing through our heart about whether it's true at all. David Watson was a well-known evangelist in the 1960s and 70s and died of cancer, much to everyone's shock and sadness. He wrote shortly before he died:

> I remember once or twice waking up about two or three in the morning with my pyjamas wringing wet with sweat. I was asking myself very basic questions – 'If I'm shortly on my way to heaven, how real is heaven? If there's really a God . . .' I was absolutely staggered that I was going right the way back to square one about one's basic beliefs. Fortunately I had worked through these questions sufficiently and they didn't last all that long. But I found I had real fears, doubts and agonies of mind.

No one is immune. But a period of doubt and even an ongoing questioning of orthodox beliefs, can be a boon to faith, because it makes us go deep. It propels us out of the comfortable shallows where our easy answers go unchallenged and gets us into deep water where we have to learn to swim again. Dostoevsky wrote, 'It is not as a child that I believe and confess Jesus Christ. My "hosanna" is born of a furnace of doubt.' Such confession of Christ is much more secure than an unexamined faith. A strong tree has deep roots. The deeper the roots, the more secure it is, even though those roots are reaching completely in the opposite direction to the tree's growth. So it is with faith. When the roots have had to travel deeply in the opposite direction to the growth, that faith is all the stronger. Questions and doubts make us hoe the ground and turn over the soil of our faith. What hopefully comes to the top is fresh dark soil ready for new planting.

There are, of course, pressures on us to be positive, confident Christians, whatever the weather, and it's particularly hard to function when the acid of doubt is eating away inside us. We're entitled to live more quietly at such times and to display vulnerability in appropriate ways. We can speak of the importance of questions if we're to understand our secular neighbour and we can preach about the treasures of darkness. We need to remember, also, that the opposite of faith isn't really doubt, but the wrong kind of certainty.

I have for a long time resonated with the words of Herbert Butterfield, a professor of history at Cambridge, who ended his book *Christianity and History* with this wise summary of the life of faith: 'Hold fast to Christ, and for the rest be totally uncommitted.'[3] If we commit ourselves to that compelling, enthralling, enigmatic preacher from Galilee, the rest will work itself out.

Tailpiece: a quote from Ian Hislop

One of the first times I ever appeared on radio, I got into a discussion about whether being rude to people was a very Christian activity. 'But you're not a Christian,' said the presenter. 'No,' I laughed. The cocks did not crow and even the pips did not go for a time check but I felt curiously disappointed with myself. At the time I was not sure whether I could be classified as a Christian or not. I did not really believe but I did not really not believe. I suppose I believed in belief. I feel much the same now. Robert Browning put the dilemma perfectly in his poem 'Bishop Blougram's Apology':

All we have gained then by our unbelief
Is a life of doubt diversified by faith
For one of faith diversified by doubt.
We call the chessboard white – we call it black.

A life of doubt diversified by faith is roughly as far as I have got, now that I've reached the age that Christ died. I don't know which colour the chessboard is. I've sat in churches thinking this is all rubbish. And at other times I have felt that this is all there is. I don't know. I don't know.

Resources

Joan Bakewell (ed.), *Belief* (London: Duckworth, 2005).

Justin Brierley, *Unbelievable: Why after ten years of talking with atheists, I'm still a Christian* (London: SPCK, 2017).

Barbara Brown Taylor, *When God is Silent: Divine language beyond words* (Norwich: Canterbury Press, 2013).

Bel Mooney, *Devout Sceptics: Conversations on faith and doubt* (London: BBC, 2003).

John Pritchard, *God Lost and Found* (London: SPCK, 2011).

Mark Yaconelli, *Disappointment, Doubt and Other Spiritual Gifts: Reflections on life and ministry* (London: SPCK, 2016).

R
Renewal

When Willie Whitelaw was Home Secretary, he was visiting a prison and stopped to ask one of the inmates what he had been sentenced for. 'I'm a contract killer,' came the reply, to which Willie Whitelaw made his standard response, 'Splendid, splendid. Keep up the good work.' It's important to listen to what's being said . . .

The Church has to listen to what society is saying to it. As congregations decline and the place of faith in public life is increasingly contested and sidelined, we can't keep on doing the same thing and hoping that the world will come to its senses and return to the good old days. We may believe deeply in what we're doing but to many in society we look like 'some kind of ecclesiastical branch of the Sealed Knot Society re-enacting events from the seventeenth century for our own enjoyment.'[1] To change the image only slightly, the wisdom of the Dakota Indians says that when you discover you are riding a dead horse, the best strategy is to dismount.

We know that the Church both locally and nationally will never be perfect. The reason is simple: it's made up of people like me. But, then, it's like our physical bodies; they aren't fully healthy either, but we get along most of the time. So does the Church, although sometimes church life can seem like a game of rugby where players ignore the ball and spend their time tackling each other, members of their own team or even people in the crowd.

I love the honesty of Nadia Bolz-Weber who wrote:

> It's my practice to welcome new people to the church by making sure they know that House for All Sinners and Saints [her Lutheran church in San Francisco at that time] will, at some point, let them down. That I will say or do something stupid and disappoint them. And then I encourage them to decide *before* that happens if they will stick around *after* it happens. If they leave, I tell them, they will miss the way God's grace comes in and fills in the cracks left behind by our brokenness. And that's too beautiful to miss.'[2]

It's a refreshing and disarming approach we might all copy.

Renewal in the Church has many elements to it – individual, corporate, conceptual, structural and missiological. Renewal could start at any one of those five places, not just at the top, but then it has to spread through the whole organism. What follows is a personal list of key principles of renewal, born of some experience, a fair bit of failure and much reflection. It makes no claim to any authority save that of a jobbing bishop who cares deeply that the Church should be renewed constantly by the refreshing wind of the Spirit. How can we steer the great ocean liner 'The Church of God' into these new waters?

See the Church as a movement more than an institution Indeed, Jesus probably never intended his followers to establish the Church as a 'thing' in itself. Institutions have to look to self-preservation through having their core beliefs enshrined in statements, constitutions and rules, but the Church of Jesus was surely intended first to be a movement of people who followed his Way to freedom. It's as if God's pilgrim people started out on the Way of Jesus with a light heart and an empty backpack, energized by the prospect of the journey, the companions, the terrain and the goal. But the people they encountered kept saying they needed to take with them various rock samples that were too valuable to leave at the roadside. *This* rock would be needed at some stage. *That* rock was one everyone picked up at some point. Bit by bit the backpack got heavier and heavier until it was a huge burden, hard even to pick up. Inevitably the question arose: was this what the journey was supposed to be about? Shall we leave the backpack at the roadside? Institutions are notorious for the way they pick up rocks and make them seem essential. Movements, on the other hand, are committed to travelling light, as Jesus instructed his friends when he sent them out on mission (Luke 10.4). The Church inevitably has to have an institutional form, but it needs to have a pilgrim heart. In a letter to his brother, Dietrich Bonhoeffer wrote:

> The renewal of the Church will come from a new type of monasticism which only has in common with the old an uncompromising allegiance to the Sermon on the Mount. It is high time men and women bonded together to do this.

If it was high time then, it's beyond time now.

Refreshing spirituality To many Christians the word 'renewal' means charismatic renewal, which has been a great gift to churches in Britain since the 1970s, giving rise to many networks such as New Wine and Soul Survivor (which has now felt God's call to step back from its large youth festivals). Through a fresh emphasis on the work of the Holy Spirit and a parallel outpouring of new music, most churches have felt the touch of this form of renewal. However spiritual renewal takes many forms and shapes. 'The inner life is called the soul, and the art of knowing it, healing it, and harmonising its forces is called spirituality.'[3]

In wider society, we live in an age of spiritual consumerism where people shop around for a 'must fit me' product that looks good and isn't too difficult to use. But the spiritual needs being expressed throughout society are real and the spiritual mood shifts in subtle ways. We need to be in touch, but not in thrall, to these mood swings. It's important to try and stay attuned to the way these needs are expressed so that we can offer the priceless gifts that come from the treasure store of Christian spirituality. One of the key gifts is that of silence, space and 'slowth'. We live in a society obsessed with speed, noise and instant results, but the way of nature is slow and silent. Christian spirituality has many resources to help this shift of mind, body and spirit. *Christian mindfulness* is first cousin to 'the sacrament of the present moment.' *Contemplative prayer* is like a deep clean of the soul. *Imaginative, sensory prayer* brings the Gospels vividly alive. *Lectio divina* lets God speak directly to the heart. *The Examen* reveals how God has been present throughout the day. *Walking slowly through the natural world* opens up God's first book (the second is Scripture). The *Jesus Prayer, praying with icons, Taizé, Iona, pilgrimage* – the list is endless. How do we as ministers enrich the church's spiritual menu so that seekers can find and the hungry be fed? (see **Prayer**).

Quality in worship Part of our failure to enchant people with the beauty of God has been because we haven't adapted our style of worship to changing times. People wanted a more participative church and we kept them sitting in rows and listening. They wanted a church that offered variety and we made them sit through the same thing again and again until they got bored.

They wanted a church that set them real tasks and challenges and we told them to keep quiet and conform. We carried on serving up the same food in the same way and never changed the menu. This is a parody, of course, and the essentials of worship – word and sacrament, story and song – don't change. But the style has to. Every service of worship has to be freshly baked. Perhaps we've forgotten that church-as-we-know-it is a very specific subculture in society, while many experimental forms of church are actually considerably closer to being church for mainstream culture. In any case, humanity is very diverse and our spiritual needs in worship are diverse too. In any one family we may well have those who like red meat, one is a vegetarian, one needs gluten-free food and one loves anything spicy. If we aim for compromise and serve up plain chicken and boiled rice, the result is insipid and tasteless. Instead, we need to enjoy diversity and attend to atmosphere and ambience, symbol and sacrament, how the story is told and how we sing our quiet alleluias. How 'liquid' is our worship? How does it flow? Above all, how does it help people to encounter God?

Deep and real The Church at its best is a place where everyone is welcome, no one is perfect and nothing is impossible. We are to be a community that raises and faces questions, lives differently, probably looks a bit odd and doesn't mind if it does. It needs to be deep and real. I knew a priest who said he felt more support and a greater sense of community in his Alcoholics Anonymous (AA) group than in his church. Others might substitute for AA group a golf club, an operatic society or a walking group. Church needs to be a place of honesty, vulnerability and celebration where the masks are off and trust reigns, a place of safety for those living with a heart close to cracking and a place of electrifying holiness for those who have been pierced by love and shown the stars. Zac's Place is a church for bikers in South Wales. It's been described as a place where chaos and disorder sit alongside community and grace, in an environment resembling an AA meeting mixed with a casualty department.[4] We may not be trying to emulate that description in our own church but it's clearly a place of reality and depth that we might echo in our own way. How do we enable our church to be real, to go deep in faith, to get out of our depth and discover what it's like to swim in inexhaustible grace?

Quick idea: images of church

Offer the group or congregation a range of phrases and images of church and invite them to respond positively or negatively to them, first in pairs or small groups and then all together. Phrases could include: 'laboratory of the Spirit', 'carnival of believers', 'orchestra of hopefuls', 'community of kingdom-builders', 'God's jazz band', 'community of grace', 'body of Christ'. Make up your own (avoiding 'love island' or 'heritage theme-park' . . .) Draw out the responses and their implications, relating them to the local situation. Then invite people to come up with their own best image in a few minutes of quiet. There could be a series of sermons as a result.

Relational, participative and inclusive Church has often been thought of primarily in terms of buildings (church, vicarage, hall, graveyard, manse), particular activities (services, homegroups, children's groups, lunch clubs) and roles (vicar, churchwarden, elder, steward, organist). A more helpful way of perceiving church is as a network of relationships gathered around a common vision. Although the spiritual temperature of the church may be hotter near the centre, anyone is welcome, whatever belief, unbelief, questioning, doubting or seeking they bring. Everyone matters as a beloved child of God and has a contribution to make to the whole. It's important that we think of each person as gifted and seeking something, rather than as the answer to our need for people to fill a rota or take on a job. Who is this special person and what does that person seek? How can we help that person be fulfilled in a pursuit of life in abundance? It's all relational, not functional. There are, nevertheless, tasks to be achieved in church life and a gentle invitation to participate is often welcome and a forerunner to faith itself. The invitation needs to be framed carefully. A volunteer at Labour HQ, looking for help with an election campaign, once telephoned James Callaghan and asked him if he'd ever thought of getting more involved in politics. He admitted to having been prime minister.

Christ-centred It sometimes takes an outsider to speak the truth with the greatest simplicity. Philip Pullman, no friend of the Church, is nevertheless prepared to call himself a 'Jesus-ite'. He once said:

> It seems to me the Archbishop of Canterbury might think it's worth saying 'I'm going to follow Jesus and anyone who wants to come with me can follow because this way leads to love and compassion and tolerance. If you don't like it, stay here, but this is the way I'm going.'[5]

This is what the Church is called to do and as ministers we're tasked with getting the followers together and caring for them on the journey. Jesus is the one who demonstrates most fully that love is the soul of the world. He gives us our grid reference, our compass bearing and our food for the journey. 'All the church has ever needed to rise from the dead,' wrote Barbara Brown Taylor, 'is memory, bread, wine, and Holy Spirit – that and care for the world.'[6] All those elements are about Jesus. I've been to some churches where Jesus hardly gets mentioned and where you have to scramble around to find a Bible – the book that tells his story. Jesus is the centre. How can we make him more visible and captivating? Christ-centred churches are usually magnetic.

Engaged with the world Martin Luther King Jr said that life's most persistent and urgent question is 'What are you doing for others?' We are not in existence to provide Sunday morning light entertainment. We're here to lay the foundations of the kingdom of God. Church is not the main thing; the kingdom is the main thing, as introduced by Jesus. This means that the Church's task is to bless, serve and challenge the world against the plumb line of the values of the kingdom (see the New Testament). The question we need to keep before the local church is therefore 'What are we doing here that makes a genuine difference to people's lives?' The other main implication of being engaged with the world around us is that it requires all of us to take seriously our 'whole-life discipleship'. Monday through Saturday is the test of our faith, not Sunday morning. How much does faith mean to us? Where does it bite? What resources do people need to live out their faith in the hard places of daily life? These are questions that many churches quietly avoid. We mustn't let ourselves off.

Structures and safety So we know what has to be done. It's about love, in many forms. Worship is giving God's love back to God. Pastoral care is giving God's love to one another. Evangelism and social action are about giving God's love to the community. Teaching and training are about giving God's love to the Church. We know what has to be done, but what is the structure we need to do this most effectively? We want to respond primarily to the mission God has given us in relation to the world and not just bend our ways to financial constraints and centralized tidiness. But we have to listen to the wind of the Spirit and what the Spirit is saying to the churches through the facts before us. In the Church of England, what's emerging for the future seems to be a mixed economy of five embodiments of church: resource churches, some stronger parish churches, festival churches to cover occasional offices and major festivals, fresh expressions of church and churches that meet as small groups in people's homes (back to the beginning). Central Church priorities need to be flexible enough to see what the Spirit is doing and then pour in the resources. And through every form of church must run a scrupulous concern for safeguarding. Our past laxity has been catching us up and society is not impressed.

So what?

Renewal of the Church at this time is like refitting a ship while still at sea. Or – changing the image – it's like ministers having to be undertakers and midwives at the same time. It's hugely complex. Bishop Alan Smithson once wrote:

> We would all like to see the Church's new clothes. What will we look like in ten years' time? Will the new clothes be like the Emperor's – non-existent? Or like the garments of Colossians 3.12 ('Clothe yourselves with compassion, kindness, humility, meekness and patience . . . Above all, clothe yourselves with love.')? It may be too soon to say, since the fabric is not yet on the loom. But since the designer of the loom is the Master Carpenter of Nazareth the end product will be a perfect fit, tailor made, for the Church and for people who are ready to grow.

We've done enough patching. Today's ministers have to start weaving new cloth according to the pattern of Christ the Weaver.

Tailpiece: on the Church of England

Why do I love it? Let me count the ways. I love it because it is patient. It does not expect the world to change in an instant or to be bludgeoned into belief, because it knows that certain things take centuries. I love it because it is kind. It is kind to welcome strangers, whatever their beliefs and shake their hands and offer them a coffee after church. I like the fact that it is not arrogant or rude. I like the fact that it does not insist on its own way but is genuinely tolerant of other religious beliefs – and none. I like the fact that it does not rejoice in wrongdoing, but quietly presents an ethical framework of kindness. I like the fact that it believes in the values of the New Testament and of St Paul's description of love, which I've just paraphrased, but also believes that it's more important to embody them than to quote them. I like the fact that it doesn't speak like a child, think like a child or reason like a child. I like the fact that it is mature enough to value faithful doubt. I like the fact that it is calm . . .[7]

Resources

Steve Aisthorpe, *The Invisible Church: Learning from the experiences of churchless Christians* (Edinburgh: St Andrew Press, 2016).

Keith Elford, *Creating the Future of the Church: A practical guide to addressing whole-system change* (London: SPCK, 2013).

David Goodhew (ed.), *Church Growth in Britain: 1980 to the present* (Farnham: Ashgate, 2012).

David Kinnaman, *Unchristian: What a new generation really thinks about Christianity* (Grand Rapids, MI: Baker Books, 2009).

Michael Volland, *The Minister as Entrepreneur: Leading and growing the Church in an age of rapid change* (London: SPCK, 2015).

David Walker, *God's Belongers: How people engage with God today and how the Church can help* (Abingdon: BRF, 2017).

Sam Wells, *A Future that's Bigger than the Past: Towards the renewal of the Church* (Norwich: Canterbury Press, 2019).

S

Self-care

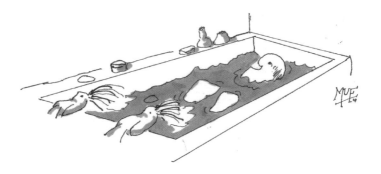

It's an ugly phrase but an important concept. We have to look after ourselves if we're to be of use to others. This chapter focuses on the self-care of the clergy but anyone involved in ministry can find themselves overworked and stressed. Churchwardens often find they've added thirty per cent to their working week. Treasurers and musicians often find they're committed to far more than they realized. It's important that such good people give themselves permission to lay down their burden if they find it's damaging their physical or spiritual health or causing grief at home. In what follows I hope those who are not clergy or authorized ministers may nevertheless be able to extract some suggestions of value for their situations too.

When I was a diocesan youth officer, I burnt out in a way that alarmed me both then and now. Running a youth weekend for 650 people among the ancient ecclesiastical buildings of Wells proved my undoing and, whereas up to that point I felt that I could tackle anything, I now knew I had limits. The experience of stress has remained vividly with me. I learnt much from it, but I don't want to repeat it.

It's good news that in job satisfaction surveys the clergy usually come somewhere near the top, but with much satisfaction comes much risk. We have to take care of ourselves too.

Look after the good news

What is it about the gospel that attracted you so much that you made it the centre of your life? What's the heart of the gospel for you? What is it you hope people will catch? Whatever that is – the attractiveness of Jesus, the unconditional love of God, forgiveness and new life, the contemplation of God – it has to be something we can articulate clearly and hold on to with joy. This is what we'll find ourselves speaking about, what others will hear and what we'll bear witness to, in whatever we do in ministry, because the way we do anything is the way we do everything. We mustn't lose the heavenly vision.

Closely related to this is another question. What is it that really fires us now in ministry and lifts our heart when we think about it? What's the passion within the passion? Is it helping people find faith, ministry with young people, taking people on pilgrimage, the study of icons, issues of peace and justice, poetry, creating fresh liturgy, medieval theologies of the atonement (perhaps not)? There'll be something that gets the juices running and where real energy is released in each one of us. If we can identify that interest and pursue it, it will be a source of joy that liberates our whole ministry. In particular, it can become a 'sixth-day ministry', that is, five days doing the day job and a sixth day developing the special interest that could be offered more widely if it's appropriate, but that in any case enlivens our own ministry. This is where our best work is done. This is what really matters to us. So, on the principle of building our ministry on our passions, what is the good news for us and what particularly gives us life now?

Look after your spirituality

Ministry is the overflow of our prayer life. If that dries up, so does our ministry; it becomes a routine turning of the ministerial and liturgical handle. We have to sincerely desire God and open the curtains of our heart to God every morning. Of course, the way we do that is as unique as God's way of loving us, but a rhythm of prayer is essential – without it becoming a legalism that fills us with guilt if we sometimes miss it.

If the day doesn't start with a focus on God, we'll never catch up. The day will take off and never stop. A parent of young children won't have much time to do this but nearly all of us can manage a prayer in the bathroom, such as a favourite of mine: 'Gracious God, I offer this day to you, the work I do, the people I meet, the pleasures and the problems, that in everything I may know the love of Christ, and be thankful.' A useful verse is from Colossians 3.17: 'Whatever you do, in word or deed, do everything in the name of the Lord Jesus, giving thanks to God the Father through him.'

However we start the day, with extended prayer or a brief offering, we have pulled back the spiritual curtains and are held in the loving gaze of God all day, a gaze that we hopefully return, practising the presence of God and punctuating the day with remembrances, with gratitude and with arrow-like intercession. As the day nears its end, we can return to our self-designated rhythm with an evening office, night prayer, recollection of the day (the Examen), a little reading or some other discipline. The day needs to be gently marinated in prayer.

The danger of being involved in serious ministry, lay or ordained, is that this dependence on God becomes routine and loses the expectancy and joy of encountering the living God. We have to go beyond the bread and butter of dutiful prayer and remember with Gregory of Nyssa that 'the most important thing is to become [remain] God's friend'. We need to be able to answer the important question, 'How do you let God love you?' So the rhythm we develop will benefit from further support from, for example, quiet days, retreats, spiritual accompaniment and festivals.

But our spirituality starts and finishes with that desire for God expressed in psalm 42: 'As a deer longs for flowing streams, so my soul longs for you, O God. My soul thirsts for God, for the living God. When shall I come and behold the face of God?' We live in the kindly gaze of God and that gaze says 'I love you'. Our joy is to return the gaze and find that it's the wellspring of our ministry.

Look after your mind

If our doctor hadn't read a medical article for years or undertaken several days' training each year to refresh his or her knowledge and keep up to date with new treatments, we would rightly be concerned. So it is with 'physicians of the soul'. We too need to keep alive intellectually. The old canard that you can tell when a minister stopped thinking by looking at the books on the shelves, isn't entirely false. It's too easy to become repetitive in ministry.

It's also too easy to become superficial. The Internet and social media have trained our brains to read a paragraph or two and then start looking around for the next diversion. We find ourselves clicking on the sidebars and the underlined links. Soon we're looking at presidential tweets or checking the weather. The Internet is doing new things to our brains and it's serious reading that's often losing out.

Ministers can't afford to let that happen. An article in *Business Insider* studied pioneers like Bill Gates, Mark Zuckerberg, Warren Buffet and Oprah Winfrey and found that most of them have a common practice of reading for at least an hour a day. This is time set aside for learning. Bill Gates reads fifty books a year, Mark Zuckerberg at least a book every two weeks, while Elon Musk grew up reading two books a day! We might not aspire to such high standards, but some regular input must surely find a place in our ministry.

Although the Internet has the problems described above, it also has its considerable strengths, making available at the touch of a mouse a huge quantity of information, alongside talks, sermons, courses and other learning opportunities. The expansion of choice is nothing short of spectacular and all of us have more at our fingertips than previous generations would have thought imaginable. The dangers and the benefits of the Internet need a careful balance.

In the parish, I put in the diary a morning every two weeks for reading. It was the first thing to go, of course, because the unexpected forever broke in, but it was symbolically important. In my latter days in my busiest ministry, I would get up early and make sure that I had 45 minutes of reading time at 7 a.m. When we're giving out, we have to be taking in if we're to have anything fresh to offer our congregations and if we're to stay alive intellectually. What do we read? It can be books recommended in church newspapers, books and articles recommended by others in ministry and journals that keep us up to date with trends in the wider culture (such as *The Economist*, *Prospect*, weekend newspapers, *Private Eye*). I would add modern novels too because they take us into worlds we wouldn't otherwise inhabit.

Above all, we want God to remain our holy fascination, for if we cease to be men and women who are eager to learn and grow in our understanding of God and the world we serve, we will increasingly find we have little to offer.

Look after your relationships

Ministry so easily leaks into everything else and we have to sustain our key relationships free of such leakage. I got married the same summer I was ordained and I fear I put too much time into caring for the rest of the world and not enough into caring for my new and lovely wife. Since then, the first thing to go into a new diary has been our holidays and, with a bit of imagination, I found that I was rarely more than ten weeks from a break. It's also valuable to book treats well ahead – concerts, theatre, trips to friends, celebration meals. If they're in the diary you can say you're booked at that time and can't fit in with someone else's schedule. Days off for stipendiary clergy could start the previous evening and give the opportunity for one or even two nights away.

There's an obvious danger of deflecting stress on to our partner, particularly in marriages that are supposed to be exemplary. Two important disciplines: keep communicating and keep short accounts.

Looking after relationships is particularly important for single people who don't have a partner at home to relax with. Work easily spills over and fills all the time available. Single people have to give themselves permission to take extra time to travel to old friends and family. The extra nights away are more than balanced by the extra time worked by most single people.

Lay Christians holding a special church role can also find themselves taken for granted in terms of time to recuperate. They will normally have a day job or other significant responsibilities but are easily expected to be available in the way that an ordained colleague would be. They need to know when to say no as well. Good relationships at home are essential to good ministry outside the home.

It's hard to maintain old friendships when weekends are major times of work. Both lay and ordained ministers need to keep an eye on these friendships and make sure contacts are maintained, visits arranged, holidays shared and so on. We work very hard in ministry and we need to be generous with ourselves when it comes to looking after our key relationships.

Look after your hobbies

Faithful ministry, generously offered, shouldn't diminish our all-round enjoyment of life. Jesus declared that he had come that we might have life and have it abundantly (John 10.10). Two rabbinic questions stay with me. Rabbi Zusya expected to be asked at the gates of heaven, not, 'Why were you not Abraham or why were you not Moses?' but, 'Why were you not Zusya?' Another rabbi expected God to ask him, 'So, did you enjoy my creation?' We have a responsibility under God to be fully our God-given selves and to enjoy in full the beauty and fascination of the world we've been given.

That includes the hobbies and interests that have nothing whatsoever to do with ministry (and therefore unlike sixth-day ministries). I have always loved it when I've discovered the range of interests and passions that ministers have, introducing me to worlds of which I had little understanding. A bishop who loved grandfather clocks, old cars, wine, singing and the violin. A priest who made superb ten-foot models of old ships. Another who was an extra in films and television dramas and one who acted as Henry VIII at Tudor feasts. It delights me to discover ministers who cycle for pleasure as well as the expected railway buffs. I love finding ministers who turn wood on a lathe and poets who turn phrases on a page.

These hobbies clean the lens that so easily becomes dominated by ministerial concerns and they re-engage us with the wider creation that God wants us to enjoy. But if there isn't any outside interest that particularly appeals to us at present, we can always call up the declaration made by George Macleod, the founder of the contemporary Iona Community. He said: 'Work isn't always required. There's such a thing as sacred idleness, the cultivation of which is now fearfully neglected.'

Quick idea: audit

Why not make these six points the basis of a regular audit of how well your own 'self-care' is going? When you go away for a quiet day, a retreat or a session with a spiritual director you could take this list. How do you:

- look after the good news?
- look after your spirituality?

- look after your mind?
- look after your relationships?
- look after your hobbies?
- look after your body?

Honest appraisal of how you're managing these aspects of life could give valuable material for reflection and that could either be reassuring or suggest new actions to take.

Look after your body

This is the point at which I ought to step aside in embarrassment. My attempts to maintain the slim, svelte-like figure of my youth have singularly failed. But I absolutely recognize the importance of a healthy body supporting a healthy mind. It's too easy to drive everywhere, giving as the reason that we have so much to do today. Moreover, walking or cycling is better for our ministry, as well as our health, because of the visibility we gain. Ministers who run or play tennis, badminton, squash, golf or five-a-side football, are keeping in good shape both physically and mentally. Failing all those, membership of a gym would probably be put on ministerial expenses in the USA.

Healthy living, including our diet, is part of our respecting God's gift to us of our bodies, those temples of the Holy Spirit. It balances our life and sharpens up our ministry. It feels good and it's enjoyable. We meet new people beyond our Christian bubble.

I'm convinced – now I have to do it.

Tailpiece: boosters

Dr Eve Poole writes of the need to manage our personal battery life:

Here is a generic list of those research-based boosters that are known to help: sleep, rest and prayer; water, bananas and low-GI foods; music, singing and dancing; beauty, joy and mindfulness; altruism, friends and family; the outdoors, views and perspective; flattery, laughter and winning.[1]

Resources

Alan Bartlett, *Vicar: Celebrating the renewal of parish ministry* (London: SPCK, 2019).

Jamie Harrison and Robert Innes (eds), *Clergy in a Complex Age: Responses to the guidelines for the professional conduct of the clergy* (London: SPCK, 2016).

Gordon Oliver, *Ministry without Madness* (London: SPCK, 2012).

Emma Percy, *What Clergy Do: Especially when it looks like nothing* (London: SPCK, 2014).

John Pritchard, *The Life and Work of a Priest* (London: SPCK, 2007).

Magdalen Smith, *Steel Angels: The personal qualities of a priest* (London: SPCK, 2014).

Tim Stead, *Mindfulness and Christian Spirituality: Making space for God* (London: SPCK, 2016).

S
Suffering

I'm writing this a few days after some members of the church family I belong to have experienced another loss more desperate than it seems possible for anyone to sustain. My mind shuts down at the thought of it. In ministry, this is very fragile territory. Emotions are paper thin and we can rip them open with the wrong words, a fatuous reassurance or a clumsy platitude. Sometimes only our silence is good enough.

Suffering is the greatest pastoral and intellectual challenge for Christians. Sometimes a church can feel buried under an avalanche of tragedies because everyone gets hurt at some point when the mountainside gives way.

> So-called normal life includes tragic loss, family breakdown, childlessness, serious illness, domestic violence, redundancy, bankruptcy, mental illness, failure, disappointment, serious accident and a host of other painful, traumatic events. Yet, in the West, when suffering comes upon us, we often think it is an anomaly.[1]

It isn't. It's what most of us experience at some time. It's what life does.

Responses

As shown in the chapter on **Death**, there are many different ways of responding.

- *Practical* This is when the community of the church needs to be mobilized to provide support, be it food, transport, babysitting or whatever is needed.
- *Emotional* In Michael Rosen's book *We're Going on a Bear Hunt*, a family encounters a variety of obstacles and each time there's a steady refrain: 'We can't go over it. We can't go under it. Oh no! We've got to go through it.'² So it is with those who suffer. They need people who'll hang around while they go through it and our ministry will often be a gentle one of presence, listening, lament and occasional touch. Things get real when you're down in life's cruel basement; it isn't a time for what Barbara Brown Taylor calls 'tabloid gossip and shopping news'.
- *Spiritual* An unfussy ministry of prayer and sacrament will be appropriate in more situations than we might imagine. When we get to places beyond normal words, sacraments can do the job for us, as can symbols – the gift of a hand cross to hang on to can be life-saving. I once gave a very ill parishioner a prayer card. She later said she couldn't even read the card but just holding it was enough; the prayer was made. Verbal prayer should never be forced on people but, with permission, simple prayers, often of the old-fashioned, vaguely familiar variety, can be a source of hope and comfort. We also need to remember that returning to church after a bereavement can be very difficult. Emotional defences, carefully built up, can be shattered by the singing of hymns or the sympathy of church friends. A planned return with a particular friend may be the best approach to take.
- *Intellectual* Looking at the intellectual problem of suffering has to be judged very precisely. It can only be offered to someone

if and when they want to engage with it. Nevertheless, it remains the most damaging blade that slides into the heart of faith and, for those victims who want to remain faithful believers, it can be the most hurtful extra dimension of their suffering. Abstruse arguments are unlikely to help at any time, but images and illustrations might be fed in carefully through conversations (see below). And, further, the issue ought to be tackled in sermons, nurture groups, teaching, blogs and elsewhere as opportunities arise.

The apologetic challenge

The actor Stephen Fry launched a spontaneous and devastating attack on belief in God when he was interviewed on an Irish television programme in 2015. Asked what he would say to God if he met him, Fry said:

> Bone cancer in children, what's that about? How dare you? How dare you create a world in which there is such misery that is not our fault? It's not right, it's utterly, utterly evil. Why should I respect a capricious, mean-minded, stupid God who creates a world that is so full of injustice and pain? The god who created this universe – if it was created by God – is quite clearly a maniac, utter maniac, totally selfish. We have to spend our lives on our knees thanking him? It's perfectly apparent he's monstrous, utterly monstrous, and deserves no respect whatsoever.[3]

It's the witness of those who have suffered grossly themselves that moves us most deeply. Elie Wiesel was a teenager who arrived at Auschwitz and saw children 'turned into wreaths of smoke beneath a silent blue sky'. He wrote, 'Never shall I forget those flames which consumed my faith for ever. Never shall I forget those moments which murdered my God and my soul and turned my dreams to dust.'[4] Each of us can add to such a charge list. A tsunami that killed a quarter of a million people on Boxing day. Three thousand people who went to work in two tall buildings in New York and never came home. My young sister-in-law who died in five days. When I was a vicar, we had two people in the parish who had leukaemia at the same time. One was a young man with a family; the other a seven-year-old girl. We had a healing ministry in the parish and we offered the same healing services, the same prayer, the same love and listening. But the young father died and the little girl lived. Why? Is God capricious? Does God have favourites?

In 1776, the philosopher David Hume made the argument rather more prosaically to insist that God could not be both good and powerful:

> Is God willing to prevent evil but not able? Then he is impotent. Is he able but not willing? Then he is malevolent. Is he both able and willing? Whence then is evil? Conclusion? God is weak, immoral or non-existent.[5]

Quick idea

There are no quick ideas for suffering. Suffering is long, hard and lonely. As Christians, and as a church, we just have to be there for people.

Three ways into the issue of suffering

When talking with people in crisis or, even later, when they're patched up but still bleeding underneath, we have to offer any of the following ways of thinking with deep humility and care. One of the most positive things we can say is 'I don't know'. Sometimes we might be able to add, 'But here are some of the things I toss around in my mind . . .'

1 It can help to think of God's way of working in the world as being from the inside out rather than the outside in Traditionally we've thought of God intervening from the outside, as if God is usually somewhere else, doing something else and just popping into the world from time to time to do god-like things. But this leaves God with those very difficult questions to answer, illustrated above, like why didn't he intervene to save six million Jews or why didn't he stop those planes flying into the twin towers? If God could have stopped those things happening *and chose not to* – for some high-minded reason to do with the greater good – then most of us would want no more to do with him because that God is monstrous.

But if God works from the inside out, we have a very different picture. Here is a God who limits him/herself in the very act of creation. He limits his power in the world because of his love. As do we all. When we create a child, we give up having an infinite range of possible ideal children; because now we have a particular, discrete child, real flesh and blood, with *this* character and not *that* one. From now on, all we can do with this child is love and suggest and persuade and argue and bribe – but we can't *make* him or her do anything, except in the most meaningless way by the use of force.

In other words, freedom is integral to any world that's worth living in. God gives us that freedom at the expense of his own control. That must apply to the physical world too, not just to the human one. Nature must be free to be natural – to be itself. Natural disasters are just that – natural. So the movement of tectonic plates must be able to happen, even if they create tsunamis; earthquakes must be able to happen, even though buildings fall on people; cells must be able to multiply badly as well as creatively, even though they give us cancer.

So God's love for creation turns out to be much more radical and dangerous than we thought. John V. Taylor wrote:

So there will be accidents and casualties by the million every step of the way. Yet with all the risks, its agonies and tragedies, there is no other conceivable environment in which responsive, self-giving love, to say nothing of courage, compassion or self-sacrifice, could have evolved. To put it in crudely human terms, the choice before God has been this or nothing.[6]

But still, we say, what about 'Ask, and it will be given to you; search, and you will find; knock, and the door will be opened for you' (Luke 11.9). I absolutely believe that to be true, but not in a simple transactional sense as if God were a divine cash machine – put in the card and you get the money; put in the prayer and you get what you want.

If we have a God who works from the inside out rather than the outside in, then we have a God who under-rules rather than over-rules. *But still God rules. God rules by the power of love.* And precisely because of the lavishness of that love, God has limited himself to work by loving persuasion, by invitation – and by *pressing every particle of creation to work to its fullest potential.* When that truly happens, when everything is perfectly aligned, we call it a miracle. Isn't the supernatural only an infinite extension of the natural?

If we think of someone we've been praying for recently, I'm sure that what we have wanted for them is the very best that love can do. Likewise, God does all that infinite love can do – no more, no less. As we pray for that person, we're praying that our love aligns with God's love and that love 'presses into' the situation ever more fully.

We don't know what almighty love can do and what it can't do. There must be limits, in a world that's been created to be free. You can't have dry rain or square circles. We have a given world, one with intrinsic limits, but also with huge possibilities. So in our ministry we encourage people to pray on. We should pray for the young father as well as the little girl. We don't know what the in-built limits of love are in this world. Our job is to pray and God will always answer, as much as love can. And where there can't be physical healing, there might be emotional, spiritual or relational answers to our prayer. 'Ask and it will be given to you,' but the 'it' is in God's hands.

2 Recognize that God's approach to the conundrum of suffering isn't so much to give answers as to enter the questions through the life and death of Jesus We look into the deep centre of suffering and find there a suffering God. People can be scalded by others saying to them 'Everything happens for a reason, we just don't know what it is,' or 'God takes those he loves.' Like hell he does, because that would be hell if we had a God like that. What God was doing was entering our suffering himself. God didn't fix the suffering of the world, but he pitched his tent in the middle of it. Jesus brought God's presence into the heart of suffering because, as Bonhoeffer knew, 'only the suffering God can help'. There may be no refuge from suffering but God's love permeates that suffering through and through and through. In Chartres Cathedral, there's a statue representing God on the seventh day of creation. Look carefully and you can see one silent tear rolling down his face. What we may be able to do as we accompany a bereaved person is gently suggest that God doesn't cause or even 'allow' suffering; he suffers suffering. 'See from his head, his hands, his feet, sorrow and love flow mingled down. Did 'ere such love and sorrow meet, or thorns compose so rich a crown.'[7]

3 Look forwards not backwards; look at what to do with this experience rather than why it happened Getting stuck on causes keeps us in the prison house, because there's no satisfying resolution to the problem. Bad things happen. Period. The decisive question is what we do with them. One of my favourite stories is of the great violinist Itzhak Perlman who uses a wheelchair after having polio as a child. On one occasion he was performing a violin concerto when one of the strings broke in the first movement. Everyone held their breath. What would he do? Astonishingly, he continued as if nothing had happened, playing through to the end with only three strings. As the tumultuous applause died away, he was called on to say a few words. Sitting there in his wheelchair he said just one thing, 'Our job is to make music with what remains.'

We'll never really explain suffering and evil by reason and logic. But that doesn't mean there isn't a response to the problem. There is a response and it's in the nature and gift of love, expressed in creativity, forgiveness, hospitality and kindness. Making music with what remains.

Tailpiece: the gift of love

An American theologian, a young mother who'd recently completed her PhD (ironically on prosperity churches) found she had stage four cancer. Kate Bowler wrote:

> When I was sure I was going to die, I didn't feel angry. I felt loved. At a time when I should have felt abandoned by God I was not reduced to ashes. I felt like I was floating, floating on the love and prayers of all those who hummed around me like worker bees, bringing notes and flowers and warm socks and quilts embroidered with words of encouragement. They came in like priests and mirrored back to me the face of Jesus.

And her conclusion about the good news of the gospel was this: 'God is here. We are loved. It is enough.'[8]

Resources

Richard Harries, *The Beauty and the Horror: Searching for God in a suffering world* (London: SPCK, 2016).

Harold S. Kushner, *When Bad Things Happen to Good People* (London: Pan Macmillan, 2002).

C. S. Lewis, *A Grief Observed* (London: Faber and Faber, 1961).

John Morris, *Suffering: If God exists, why doesn't he stop it?* (Alresford: John Hunt Publishing, 2015).

Stephen Oliver (ed.), *Inside Grief* (London: SPCK, 2013).

John V. Taylor, *The Christlike God* (London: SCM Press, 1992).

David Watson, *Fear No Evil* (London: Hodder & Stoughton, 1984)

T
Teaching

"Once God is God....Twice God is..."

The third-century Chinese sage Chuang-Tsu said, 'If you are thinking a year ahead, sow seed. If you are thinking ten years ahead, plant a tree. If you are thinking a hundred years ahead, educate the people.'

Theologically, we are not a well-taught Church. That isn't surprising when the main diet for the majority of churchgoers is a ten-minute sermon once every week or two (or three). That doesn't make for a well-informed laity. The result, said by Dorothy Sayers years ago, was that 'the average Christian is as well equipped to meet an aggressive atheist as a boy with a pea-shooter is to meet a tank'.

Many of those called to be lay or ordained ministers have had two or three years of good-quality theological education. We have so much to offer. But it doesn't seem to happen. I want to reclaim the teaching responsibility of ministers as a task that is of the utmost importance, one that contributes so much to the health of the Church.

There are teaching opportunties that are open to others in their local churches as well, such as homegroup leaders, those involved in children's groups, people called to give occasional talks and others. Let's have a look.

Problems to overcome

Resistance by the 'customers' People lead lives of acute busyness. There has to be some clear added value from a new activity if it's to be squeezed into the bulging diary. We need to make the case that although online shopping can be useful, learning about faith can be life changing. But we have to design our learning opportunities sympathetically to take account of the overfull nature of many lives – a Saturday morning, an adult forum on Sunday morning before or after a service, an hour over breakfast, an hour straight after work, online learning. In other words, whatever fits.

Feelings of inadequacy These feelings lie in both teachers and learners. Ministers are often strangely reluctant to risk sharing their knowledge for fear of it being found out that they were never quite as clear as they would have liked about, for example, the synoptic problem or the arguments for the existence of God. Learners are often anxious that the scale of their confusion is cavernous and will be shown up. We have to reassure both ourselves and our fellow Christians that we're all learners in God's school of faith.

Where do we start? This is where market research comes in (a posh phrase for chatting to the right people). Find out if they would like input on the Bible, basic beliefs, prayer and the spiritual journey, Christian approaches to ethical issues, faith and politics, science and religion, parenting as a Christian or other areas. In other words, what part of the pond do they want to fish in? Then comes the question of design. Do people want a single session (on leading intercessions or divine guidance) or a course over four evenings (a Bible overview, a fun run through Church history) or a weekend away (on prayer or mission)? It starts with talking and listening.

Resources There are loads; no excuses (see 'Resources' at the end of this chapter for a few examples to get you started).

Learning styles

This is an area where there's usually a good deal for us to learn as teachers and facilitators. We mustn't look at the congregation and think they all learn in the same way, that is, the way we ourselves learn. We're much more diverse than that. One approach will thoroughly engage some and leave others counting the cracks in the ceiling. Another approach will excite one group and seem to others like scratching nails down a blackboard. We have to think about who's coming to learn, how they seem to engage with new things and how to offer a variety of learning styles, some of which may not be natural to us.

Here are two approaches to the varied ways we learn.

Barbe's VAK Learning Styles

Walter Barbe's research suggested that people fall into three discernible groups: learners who process information best by seeing (visual learners), by listening (audio learners) and by doing (kinaesthetic learners). Visual learners prefer displays, maps, graphs, photographs – and they tend to look upwards when they're thinking. Audio learners prefer lectures, discussions, podcasts, repetition, summaries – and they tilt their heads when concentrating. Kinesthetic learners prefer touch, physical activity, visits, reacting in a sensory way to their environment – they have difficulty sitting still through long sessions. You can see how a variety of approaches would be needed for a truly effective learning experience. Across the population, research suggests that 30 per cent favour visual learning, 25 per cent audio, 15 per cent kinaesthetic and 30 per cent a mix.

How varied was the last teaching/learning experience you taught or attended?

Honey and Mumford Learning Styles

Peter Honey and Alan Mumford developed their theory from David Kolb's influential work on experiential learning. They identified four different styles of learning: activist, theorist, reflector and pragmatist. *Activists* (obviously) take action and get involved in new things; they approach new tasks eagerly. They learn best through teamwork, role play, competitions and challenges. *Theorists* think carefully about situations, preferring to work within a given system or model rather than to be freshly creative. They respond well to statistics, compiling evidence and asking questions. *Reflectors* like to step back and learn by observation rather than by jumping into action or entering into discussion. They take time to mull things over and learn best through research, interviews, questionnaires, feedback and observation. *Pragmatists* prefer to apply knowledge and theories to the world around them. They learn by testing, experimenting and solving problems. Discussion is for others; they want to get on and try something out.

Can you apply those categories to some of the people you know? How would you run, say, a Bible overview session for them?

Quick idea: a working group

A working group can help to take the educational task out of the shadowy domain of the minister's study and share it with a working group of people with an interest in Christian growth. The group can toss ideas around and carry through learning projects. Three or four people are all that are needed, including a minister. Their task is to help the church learn in whatever ways are best.

Putting it into practice

There are various possibilities for taking forward the educational life of a church. Larger churches will be able to think bigger, but smaller churches can be imaginative and 'light touch', tailoring their ideas in more personal ways.

Sermons

These are still a front-line opportunity for people to learn, but it means being more intentional in planning sermon courses – and in preparing the sermons to handle the material clearly and imaginatively. In some churches, the sermon slot can be used for small-group discussion, an interview or a question-and-answer session. Remember the visual learners and the possibility of using so much that's now available on the Internet – film clips, news stories, interviews.

Dimensions of belonging

There's still wisdom in our thinking of Christians having four dimensions to their relationship with God and the Church. We relate to God *individually* and personally – the crucial one to one. Then a *small group* enables us to find friendship and opportunity to grow, to question and to pray with others. The third dimension is the *congregation* where we are nurtured in worship and equipped for mission; the fourth is the *celebration* event at area, regional or national level that gives us the encouragement of the bigger occasion at a summer festival such as New Wine, a cathedral or a conference. Are members of the church you serve given opportunities and encouragement at each of those levels?

Homegroups

Homegroups are still vital building blocks in a teaching and learning policy. They're a place for people to find their feet in faith, to learn and grow. The danger, of course, is that they become sterile, with the same members riding the same hobby horses over the same ground (and stumbling at the same fences). An important element of a successful homegroup is 'output'. Does the heat and light of the group have any impact outside itself in the wider life of the church or in service to others? This can rescue a group from sterility by opening an escape hatch for the energy generated inside. It's good to put this on every homegroup agenda.

Beginners groups

Just as homegroups need a point of output, so the whole Church needs a point of input, that is, a way into faith for beginners, explorers and enquirers. Every church or group of churches needs a regular way in of this kind, a group to which those who brush up against the church can be referred (see 'Resources' below).

Niche groups

People love gathering around common passions and – in this context – these groups don't have to be overtly religious. Too much full-frontal religion can be wearying. We can explore profound themes of life and faith through art, poetry, novels, music and more to everyone's enjoyment and enlightenment. Such groups can have short as well as longer runs. Ambitious churches might even have a Theology Group to tackle heavier issues or weightier books (for which the offer of a glass of wine might help things along).

Lecture courses

Some churches or groups of churches put on a series of annual lectures where the larger scale enables them to invite more high-profile speakers. With careful choice of subjects and speakers, this can be a highlight of the learning year. Equally, I found in one context that we had sufficient expertise ourselves across the town that we could run three parallel four-session courses once or twice a year. The uptake demonstrated how much they were valued.

Weekend and day courses

Church weekends have become too expensive for many churches but the value of time away, thinking, eating, sleeping and laughing together is enormous. Failing that, a church day away or a church weekend at home can pick up some of the same benefits. Failing even that, a Saturday morning giving concentrated attention to a topic can achieve a lot more than a ten-minute sermon.

Church themes

As an example, I was once vicar of a church where we had a Lenten theme entitled 'Read, *Mark*, Learn', based on the Gospel of that name. At the start of Lent, everyone was given a copy of Mark's Gospel with a reading plan. There was a homegroup course, a sermon course, children's activities, visual displays and more, all of which gave coherence to an important theme and introduced regular reading of the Bible to many who hadn't tried it before. Mark became an old friend.

Mentoring

It can be very valuable to take under our wing someone who is hungry to learn and grow, and to contract to meet them regularly in a coffee shop or church lounge in order to support their growth. One-to-one mentoring gives the learner access to a quality of wisdom and experience for which they will always be grateful. It's time-intensive but deeply rewarding. One possible downside to note, sadly, is what has come to be called 'spiritual abuse' if the mentoring is too directive and the one being mentored is restricted in making a free response.

Diocesan/wider church learning

Every Anglican diocese and every denomination has a variety of learning opportunities through courses, conferences, hubs, learning platforms, chat rooms and so on. Use of the Internet and social media has opened up immense riches to the Church. Lay and ordained ministers have a special task in encouraging these opportunities through making connections and offering suggestions to individuals. We have to be those who intentionally signpost the good things on offer.

Book recommendations

This is another signposting task for ministers. We ourselves are still reading, hopefully, so we'll know some of the scene as far as good, up-to-date Christian books appropriate for our congregation are concerned. Verbal recommendations from the pulpit and in the news-sheet are of great value, but best of all is the personal one-to-one recommendation. We might even buy the book for someone (or lend it . . .).

Tailpiece: the Church's commitment to education

In 1811, Joshua Watson, an entrepreneurial lay Christian with a background as a wine merchant, had two good friends at his house for coffee. They had met to discuss how best they could serve the needs of the poor and the result was the National Society for Promoting the Education of the Poor, the aim of which was to establish a church school in every parish in the kingdom. By 1851 there were 17,000 such schools. It was only in 1870 that one of the great Education Acts brought in 'state' education to work alongside church schools. In the present day, with amalgamations and rationalization, there are nearly five thousand Church of England schools, including a quarter of the primary schools in England and Wales, educating nearly a million children. These schools are committed to being inclusive yet distinctive in their ethos and are determined to offer first-rate holistic education to every child. The Church's commitment to education goes back to its earliest days. In England, The King's School, Canterbury, claims a line right back to the arrival of Augustine in AD 597. The monasteries were the earliest regular providers of education and the public schools of the fifteenth century and thereafter were nearly all established by the Church in one way or another. The Church's commitment to teaching and learning is deep and long.

Resources

Church House Publishing, *Pilgrim: A course for the Christian journey* (London: CHP) (available online at: <www.chpublishing.co.uk>).

Grove Books (<www.grovebooks.co.uk>) has a growing Education series. For example, Margaret Cooling and Trevor Cooling, *Distinctively Christian Learning* (Cambridge: Grove Books, 2013).

SPCK has a new go-to site for homegroup leaders. See: <www.spckpublishing. co.uk/home-groups>.

All dioceses will have something like a digital learning platform signposting courses, events and opportunities. For example, see: <https://learning.leeds. anglican.org>).

Opportunities for distance-learning Christian study programmes through colleges and universities are vast. Search the Internet.

U

Unity

Christians churches have a horrible habit of splitting up. If a group decides they have a purer understanding of the faith than their fellow worshippers, the temptation is to go off and set up a new church with new conventions and shibboleths. It's been going on for centuries and shows no sign of slowing down, even though the major breaks (Catholic/Orthodox in the Great Schism of 1054, Catholic/Protestant in the sixteenth-century Reformation) are things of the past. Some observers put the number of denominations in the tens of thousands and although these figures are contentious, most of us can see in our towns and cities the sad wreckage of other splits (Anglican/Methodist, Wesleyan/Primitive Methodist, Pentecostal/better Pentecostal). This is in spite of the fact there's no such thing as a Methodist or Roman Catholic way of loving people and no Baptist or Anglican way of clothing the naked or visiting prisoners.

Tragically, modern-day splits often seem to have at their heart issues of biblical interpretation and yet it's in the Bible that we see the clearest expression of the will of Christ for Christian unity. John 17 glows with that desire. 'I ask ... that they may all be one. As you, Father, are in me and I am in you, may they also be in us, so that the world may believe ...' (John 17.20–21). Paul, too, spent much of his energy trying to hold churches

together when Gnostics, Judaizers, heretics and egotists sought
to carve out their tiny empires. I remember a preacher spending
most of a sermon on Christian unity tearing up a piece of paper
into smaller and smaller pieces as he illustrated the way we
Christians have thought to know better than Jesus.

Mark Oakley illustrates the problem vividly:

> Imagine if, instead of Communion, the Church had decided
> to centre the Sunday and daily services around the washing
> of feet command instead of the bread and wine command.
> Just imagine what we would have made of it. We would be
> having arguments over which foot should be washed, right
> or left, and there would be the Church of the Left Footers
> and the Communion of the Right Footers, we would have
> synods on whether the water should be cold or hot or,
> if Anglican, probably lukewarm. We'd be fighting over
> whether women can wash feet, whether gay people can
> have their feet washed . . .'[1]

The trouble is that, in much of the contemporary Church, enthusiasm for unity feels like a minority sport. It's like tiddlywinks
trying to get on to prime-time television. How have we fallen
not only from the heady days of church unity schemes but, more
importantly, from the explicit request of Jesus?

We can see the problem clearly enough but in churches
absorbed in the struggle to survive, grow or manage internal conflict, working together with other churches feels like the icing on
the cake rather than a key ingredient of the cake. What can we do?

There's a Sufi saying that you think because you understand
the meaning of one you must understand the meaning of two,
because one and one makes two. But, they say, you must also
understand the meaning of 'and' in the phrase 'one *and* one'. Our
'and' is God the Holy Spirit who delights in wholeness and turns
'one and one' into 'us'.

The torn garment of Christ

If the garment of Christ is torn, mending it won't be easy because the fabric is old and precious. We need a lot of love and patience when working with fabric that's worn and thin. What we have to believe is that although it will never be the same as it was, it can have a different beauty because so many people have cared for it.

In 1966, Pope Paul VI and Archbishop Michael Ramsey met in Rome. They signed a declaration affirming their desire for unity. Then the Pope asked the Archbishop to take off his episcopal ring and he slipped on to Michael Ramsey's finger his own ring, the one he'd worn as Archbishop of Milan. Michael Ramsey wept and he wore the ring for the rest of his life. Such gestures are very important when we're dealing with the precious, torn fabric of a divided Church.

To change the image, perhaps the key starting point in our search for unity, is to review the very source of our life as Christians. In what direction are we looking? Rowan Williams puts it with characteristic elegance:

> Unity exists fundamentally in a shared gazing towards Christ, and through Christ looking into the mystery of the Father. If we believe our unity comes from that looking together into a mystery, occasionally nudging each other to say, 'Look at that!', we can perhaps recognise that the unity we enjoy is not first and foremost an institutional matter; it's the common direction in which we strive to look.[2]

Perhaps we now have the elements of a strategy. First, change where we look. Then change what we do. Then change the structures around what we do. That sounds about right. And it highlights another core issue – that diversity is just as valuable as structural unity. We don't have to even everything out to a bland commonality. Anglicans bring ordered worship and a concern for the whole community; Methodists bring their concern for social justice; Baptists bring their fellowship and commitment; Presbyterians bring their love of Scripture; Pentecostals bring their enthusiasm and Quakers their calm; Roman Catholics show how everything centres on the Eucharist. Isn't diversity fun? Wouldn't structural union strangle much of that?

It might, but mission wouldn't.

Quick idea: swap shop

How about a swap shop of ideas between churches. One evening or Saturday morning have a session where each church brings at least two things they do well – one that might be copied by other churches and another that they're simply proud of. There could be a mix of presentations and time to wander around stalls that illustrate the activity, programme or event they have on display. Each stall would therefore need knowledgeable staffing. The range of displays could be enormous: from toddler groups to lunch clubs, websites to young bell-ringers, baptism preparation to church reordering, a church shop on the high street to a church-based reading group, outdoor clubs to local and overseas pilgrimages. Everyone would learn something and some would be inspired.

Making the most of working together

The prospect of a Churches Together meeting rarely sets the pulse racing. But it might depend on what people are planning.

- *Mission* We gather best around mission-based activity. That activity could be evangelism, teaching or social action but it offers people from many denominations something they believe in for itself rather than something added to the church agenda as 'ecumenism'. Notable successes have been chalked up in recent years around Street Pastors, night shelters, food banks and Church Action on Poverty with projects on debt.

In each of these cases, the activity hasn't been confined to the church bubble; it's been visible and beneficial to the wider community and won the community's admiration. Mission of this nature makes a difference and it makes new friends in other churches too. The Thy Kingdom Come annual initiative for prayer in the period from Ascension to Pentecost has become a powerful tool of prayer for mission.

- *Worship* Some special events keep coming around when cross-denominational worship is expected: Good Friday Walks of Witness, the Week of Prayer for Christian Unity, Remembrance Sunday, civic or national celebrations. What can prevent these being a tired rehash of the service that, to all intents and purposes, died last century is the imagination of those who devise the worship. The Walk of Witness could become a street-based Passion Play; the Week of Prayer for Christian Unity could be a giant Messy Church or a teaching or training day on a topic in which all the churches have an interest; civic or national celebrations could be a community festival with main stage, children's events, sporting opportunities, giant TV screen and hotdogs. But, I have to admit, it all depends on the ministers of the different churches having the commitment and energy to lead their congregations into these more adventurous territories.

- *Teaching and learning* The tradition of joint homegroups in Lent lives long and dies hard, but these groups do tend mainly to gather the 'ecumaniacs'. We could be braver. One town set up Adult Christian Education (ACE) courses twice a year, running three courses concurrently on biblical, spiritual and culture-related courses (science and religion, ethics and so on). Some churches by their space, technical know-how and imagination lend themselves more than others to major day conferences. The ecumenical secret here is to involve other churches early enough for them to have 'bought in' to the project.

- *Leaders' breakfasts and lunches* In these days when 'brand' has become increasingly significant, the leaders of a brand of churches often get together to eat, pray and support one another. Leadership can be lonely and these gatherings can be much valued as relationships deepen. When I was a curate in Birmingham, the staff team of our Anglican church met the staff team of a large United Reformed Church for Bible study and fellowship every other Monday morning and we grew together to our great mutual benefit.

• *Institutional unity* This comes last on the list not because it's unimportant but because it's meaningless unless the previous joint activities are happening. Local ecumenical partnerships have declined in popularity partly because they can involve painful levels of complexity as different church polities try to work together. The key is to find the simplicity within the complexity and make sure that simplicity always takes priority. Perhaps that applies to ecumenical structures too – effective tools for mission should flow naturally and need a minimum of complexity.

Ministers, lay and ordained, are ultimately vital if ecumenical activity is to flourish. Ecumenically motivated lay people can do a huge amount but if the leaders aren't keen, there's a limit to how far things will move. Most members of congregations are committed to the local church and might be persuaded to be interested in the 'diocesan' or national level in addition. It's the trans-local or local area that gets squeezed. Leadership is therefore crucial, and everybody has to have bought a ticket because, for example, one less-than-keen minister can undo years of good cooperation. The chemistry has to be right and people must be willing to be committed.

But in the end, surely God will have his way. The Great Church will emerge (though probably not this side of the Parousia and then it won't be necessary). Until then, however, we can at least lay the foundations and love our neighbours as ourselves.

I'll admit, I've used the following story in another book, but it's too good not to use again. The 'I' is not me . . .

Tailpiece: the man on the bridge

I was walking across a bridge one day and I saw a man standing on the edge, about to jump off. So I ran over and said, 'Stop! Don't do it!'

He said, 'Why shouldn't I?'

I said, 'There's so much to live for.'

He said, 'Like what?'

I said, 'Well, are you religious or atheist?'

He said, 'Religious.'

I said, 'Me too. Are you Christian or Buddhist?'

He said, 'Christian.'

I said, 'Me too. Are you Catholic or Protestant?'

He said, 'Protestant.'

I said, 'Me too. Are you Anglican or Baptist?'

He said, 'Baptist.'

I said, 'Wow! Me too! Are you Baptist Church of God or Baptist Church of the Lord?'

He said, 'Baptist Church of God.'

I said, 'Me too! Are you Original Baptist Church of God or are you Reformed Baptist Church of God?'

He said, 'Reformed Baptist Church of God!'

I said, 'Me too! Are you Reformed Baptist Church of God, reformation of 1879, or Reformed Baptist Church of God, reformation of 1915?'

He said, 'Reformed Baptist Church of God, reformation of 1915.'

I said, 'Die, heretic' and pushed him off the bridge.

Resources

Churches Together in Britain and Ireland (<www.ctbi.org.uk>).
Thy Kingdom Come (<www.thykingdomcome.global>).

V

Vocation

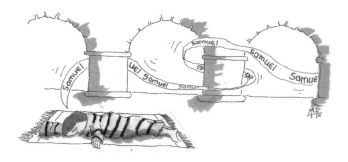

The idea of a Christian vocation easily gets diverted into well-established routes such as ordination or authorized lay ministry. But vocation is in fact a much broader concept, involving a conviction about a choice or direction of travel in any person's ministry as a Christian. Ordained ministry is only one very specific route.

To those of us who are called to ordained or lay ministry, our vocation is a precious gift to be handled with care. It probably came to us unexpectedly when we found it hanging up in the wardrobe. We tried it on for size and it felt odd, so we put it away. Then someone else said we had looked good in it, so we got it out again. Finally, we got to wear it with something approaching confidence and the Church approved, but always we wonder whether it really suits us. 'Do I look good in this?'

I've never taken on a new role in the Church without feeling out of my depth and that this will be the time when they'll finally rumble me. We can all find ourselves faced with self-doubt and the challenge of 'who do you think you are?' The more important question, of course, is 'who does God think you are?' If we listen deeply, we'll hear the answer, 'You are my much-loved child. I'm thrilled to bits with you and I want you to flourish.'

So when it comes to vocation, it's God's voice we need to hear and, in particular, where God's voice chimes with our deepest joy. Henri Nouwen defines vocation as 'where our deepest desires align with God's deep desire'. And Frederick Buechner says something similar: it's 'where our deep gladness meets the world's deep need'.

Vocation is about alignment, not achievement. It's not about our ego. It's not even about our making a decision. Decisions involve looking at goals and options, pros and cons and coming to a rational conclusion. Vocation is about being called by Another and recognising the divine harmony when it emerges from the cacophony of other sounds that invade our lives.

The alignment of our lives with God's purposes is best summed up in Paul's beautiful description of our true spiritual location: we are 'hidden with Christ in God' (Colossians 3.3). 'It is no longer I who live but Christ who lives in me' (Galatians 2.20). That's the starting place for our vocation – Christ within. But Christ within has to be balanced by Christ without, that is, Christ in his Church, because the wider Church has to recognize and confirm the call through its leadership.

Calling

For any Christian there are various calls that God may put on our lives.

The call to be fully ourselves

In Blackpool Tower there's a room with curved mirrors that make us look ridiculously fat, thin, round or hideous. In real life we too can find that we're accepting the distorted images of ourselves given by the curved mirrors held up to us by society, parents, friends, school or the media. We have to reclaim our true image and recover our own divine reflection, our own gifted life, made in the image of God. Our first call, then, is to inhabit fully the unique person God has made us to be. When we inhabit our true selves, we feel released, free, enlarged and at home in the world.

The call to be a disciple of Jesus

There is no better or higher calling. When Archbishop Justin Welby discovered not long ago that the person he had thought was his father, was not in fact a genetic match, he said simply but profoundly that his identity rested in Jesus Christ and nothing had changed in that respect. This life-defining call to be a disciple is a challenge to follow Jesus wherever that leads and to be 'covered in the dust of our rabbi', just as young trainee rabbis would literally follow their distinguished leader all day, see what they did and get covered in middle-eastern dust. Following Jesus is a thrilling way to live. When we have set our compass on Jesus, everything else becomes a matter of faithful obedience.

The call to serve

As we follow Jesus more closely, it's likely that we'll experience a call to some form of service in the Church or the wider community. Relevant questions to ask might then be: Does this prospect excite me? Is there a real need for this or is it mostly my ego speaking? Does this fit my skillset or could I develop this skill? Am I actually fulfilling my vocation in my work role? Sometimes we feel bound to take on some responsibility because no one else will come forward and the job is vital, but if that's the case we should take it on for a strictly limited period and make a priority of finding and training a successor.

The call to an authorized ministry

This 'vocation within a vocation within a vocation' is usually licensed in some way, at an appropriate level. As such, it isn't better than being a day-to-day disciple, just more clear-cut, with a name, a job description and a line of accountability. I hope we never get over the sense of privilege that should rightly accompany such a calling. I never lead a Eucharist without a sense of awe and gratitude. I'm always disappointed when I encounter people in recognized ministry who haven't outgrown silliness to do with status, clothing or general religiosity. We're not here to play religious games in a pious bubble. We have serious, joyful ministry to pursue. And one of our roles now is to look for our successors. We need to be intentional about looking around prayerfully to find other people who God might be calling to focused, recognized ministries.

Growth in ministry
Having established that we have a variety of callings, we need to look at how these callings change and grow. Vocation is a moving target and we have to keep adjusting our vision. There's an enduring task but a changing context. What is God calling me to explore now? How have my experiences so far fitted me for a new form or context of ministry? What more do I need to learn to be faithful now, in this new present time? We have to pour the liquid gold of the gospel into new moulds for new times and that calls for different priorities and skills.

I've written elsewhere about the central concerns of ordained ministry as the glory of God, the pain of the world and the renewal of the Church (see 'Resources' below). The same is true of any Christian calling, with different emphases. It's like three colours (gold, red and green) being deployed on the canvas of ministry in different ways. The core task remains, but the changing context is bound to ask for flexibility and reskilling in ministry.

> **Quick idea: skills and opportunities audit**
> Members of the congregation might be asked over a four-week period to fill in a form with two sections. One section gives open space for members to note skills or interests they have that they

might be prepared to offer. It's fascinating what turns up! The other section lists the huge range of activities in and beyond the Church to which this church is committed. This could be everything from the food bank to the flower rota. Members are asked to tick as many as they have even a remote interest in pursuing. It should be made clear that this is just for background information and no commitments are being asked for. What might emerge is a reservoir of interest in certain activities and a wonderful list of skills of which no one was previously aware, but could prove extremely useful later.

Rough water in our vocation

It would be surprising if all of us involved in following the way of Jesus did not, at some stage, hit a time of complexity and turbulence. That was certainly Jesus' experience. We start with energy and high hopes. We might make mistakes but people are forgiving and know that it's early days. Our Christian journey leads us further and deeper than we'd ever imagined. We see more of the scale of Christian service, the rich opportunities and the need to learn more. It's demanding and satisfying, fascinating and stretching, and we can roll along fairly happily doing this for a long time.

What we're less happy about is the appearance of rough water.

This isn't just the experience of being let down by others or finding the job more demanding than we ever imagined. That's discouraging but it's not insuperable. What I'm concerned about here are the rough patches that affect our relationship with God, the source of our calling. This turbulence can take various forms.

- Our own life gets tough for various personal reasons and because we're a unity of body-mind-spirit and not a collection of different boxes, it means that when one part of us suffers, so does the rest. Ministry becomes a struggle.
- We simply get weary of another Sunday morning, another

act of worship, another homegroup, another Harvest, another church council. The freshness has gone; the living reality of faith has worn thin. We keep turning the handle but frankly, we're bored.

- The Church is a place of disappointment, locally and nationally or both. It's out of touch, resistant to change, a place of argument and conflict. Congregations are declining, we're always trying to raise money, church isn't different enough, it isn't spiritual enough and it isn't *enough* of anything. We try to put a brave face on it but if we're honest, it feels as if the Church is on life support.

- The culture is relentlessly secular, hostile to religion or dismissive of it as childish. It becomes hard to represent belief when over half the population claims to have no religion and the cultured despisers of religion rule the media. The God hypothesis is beginning to look increasingly weak. Put simply, it's a battle to believe.

- God has maintained radio-silence for a very long time. It's all very well saying that absence of evidence isn't evidence of absence, but we've been talking into a void for too long. Any loving Father would have picked up the phone by now.

- We've been called to the apophatic way, beyond words, images and feelings, and into the dark country where all we can do is hunker down and wait, looking into the darkness with longing and patient faith. But to be honest, we don't actually want to be St John of the Cross, thank you very much.

However we account for it, this is rough water for our vocation as a Christian and an active member of a church. And it feels even rougher because so much of us is invested in it. This has been our core community, this faith has been the mainstay of our life, the plumb line of our values, and these people are my best friends.

So what can we do about it? Without going into detail, here are some headlines.

Take a break Don't beat yourself up but step off the train for a while and sit in the station and rest.

Phone a friend You'll know who can bear the weight.

Stay in the structures Hold on to the systems that support you – that's why they're there. For example, if you're used to daily reading of the Bible or saying the daily office, keep doing it. Frameworks matter; they hold us together.

Keep praying Jesus did, even on the cross. Go back to safe ground spiritually or on to new territory but keep the lines open.

Take Communion It bypasses analysis and goes straight to the soul.

Read Two types of book are recommended – one for the spirit (not the mind) and one easy-read novel.

Go outside Nature is healing and gets you out of your head-stuff.

Try something new Go on pilgrimage, explore art and the Gospels, sit in silence for ten minutes a day, read a new author, go to a different service.

Be patient Rushed decisions are usually wrong.
There may be longer reconstruction work to be done but these are starters. The exciting thing is that in the long run, turbulence of this nature can lead to a breakthrough into a deeper, richer and more secure faith. It can take us into a second simplicity on the far side of complexity, so that our faith isn't naïve – it's been through fire.

Such a faith might be less strident, less binary and less activist. It might be more accepting of paradox and mystery and other people's views. It's likely to be relaxed with questions and doubt, more reflective and curious. The opposite of a strong faith, remember, isn't doubt; it's unassailable certainty. Doubt is a healthy, humble response to questions so huge as to be mind-bending. This post-rough-water faith lies deeper in the participant than mere belief. Belief can be knocked about; faith is an entwining of the divine and the human so complete that it's likely to be lifelong (barring more turbulence of course).

Next?

Ordained stipendiary ministers are faced at regular intervals with a question about moving on. It might come up in a ministerial review conversation, after a sabbatical, when friends are moving on or simply when an inner time clock seems to be ticking and indicating change. For lay ministers it may be different because they aren't involved in the Church 'career' pathway in the same way, but regular reviews are still important to evaluate the emphases of their ministry. Volunteers too may come to a point of decision – is it time to move on from a long-held ministry? Is it time for a new eye on the job and for me to stretch myself against some other task?

I've never spent more than eight years in a post but there's enormous value in long ministries when communities build up trust in a minister over time and long experience, and families can entrust births, marriages and deaths to the same person. The length of a ministry shouldn't reflect society's twitchy attitude to commitment, but rather be seen as God's business. It's God's call, not a formula.

But if that's the case, how in practice can any of us discern God's guidance? It's not magic. We don't turn off our God-given common sense. When I pray for guidance, it's a bit like me putting on a pair of glasses to help me see better. It would be nonsense to assume that because I've put the glasses on, I could now close my eyes. I still use my ordinary sight but it's enhanced by the glasses. Similarly with guidance: we use our natural God-given intelligence, enhanced by divine grace.

But what do we look for? Here's a simple list.

- Deep convictions or the ideas that come to us as 'loud thoughts' need to be heard.
- What is it that keeps coming to mind as you pray and read Scripture?
- What do wise friends say? You know whose thoughts you value.
- What do circumstances say? Doors close and others open. Practical family concerns are crucial too.
- What do your instincts say? A wise spiritual director said to me as I took on a major new post, 'Trust your instincts.' We can try to get beneath the surface agitation of the water to the deeper levels where our trusted instincts lie.

A last thought: there isn't a right or wrong answer to the question of discerning a way forward. It isn't the case that if we make a 'wrong' decision, God will hold it against us and life will turn out badly. God uses and works with whatever we decide. It's the continuous process of redemption to which God is constantly committed, pressing all of creation – and all our decision-making – towards its furthest and fullest potential.

Tailpiece: St Francis

At the end of his life St Francis said, 'I have done what is mine; may Christ teach you what is yours.'

So what is yours? Where does your deepest desire align with God's deep desire? Or where does your deep gladness meet the world's deep need?

V Vocation

Resources

'Setting God's People Free' is an initiative across the Church of England to enable the complementary roles and vocations of clergy and lay people. See: <www.churchofengland.org/SGPF>.

Alan Bartlett, *Vicar: Celebrating the renewal of parish ministry* (London: SPCK, 2019).

Francis Dewar, *Called or Collared? An alternative approach to vocation* (London: SPCK, 2000).

Emma Percy, *What Clergy Do: especially when it looks like nothing* (London: SPCK, 2014).

John Pritchard, *God Lost and Found* (London: SPCK, 2011).

John Pritchard, *The Life and Work of a Priest* (London: SPCK, 2007).

Graham Tomlin, *The Widening Circle: Priesthood as God's way of blessing the world* (London: SPCK, 2014).

W
Worship

I'm writing this during a retreat that I'm leading for a religious community. We're in chapel six times a day, never knowingly diverging from the worship book. I've been here four days and I haven't sung anything yet. At the same time, I'm reading about young people going in their tens of thousands to twenty-five years of the festival Soul Survivor where worship songs are sung with high energy and at great volume. I have another book with me by an American Lutheran pastor who describes herself as a 'sarcastic, heavily tattooed, angry person who swears like a truck driver', but the worship in her church is imaginatively liturgical, full of ancient symbolism in twenty-first century clothing. At the same time, it's summer and my heart wants to be in Taizé revelling in the rich simplicity of its music and prayer that goes on gently long after bedtime.

It's all worship. It's the multicoloured, fabulously varied offering we bring to God, not because God needs it but because it connects us to our Source and gives pleasure to both worshipper and Worshipped. Worship is offering all that we are to all that God has revealed him/herself to be. It's a time of holy vulnerability when we're broken open to God, to one another and to the world's needs. We interrupt our preoccupation with ourselves for once and attend to the presence of God. And it's anything but uniform.

So how can anything written here be of any use, given how varied our offerings of worship are? All I can do is suggest some of the principles that it seems to me might be helpful as we fulfil our role as leaders of worship, if such we are, lay or ordained, in contexts formal and informal.

Who is worship for?

God

It's not because God is an egomaniac who needs constant affirmation but because God loves us and knows our deepest need is to be embraced by that love. Worship draws us into union with God and that gives God as much pleasure as it does us.

The congregation

Obviously. But it's because we've recognized that worship is a vital part of our nature, 'as much as the desire to build houses and cultivate the land, to marry and have children, and read books and sing songs'.[1] And for those who have been run over by 'the Hound' of heaven, worship is as natural as pillow talk between lovers.

The stranger

When I see a new person in church, my view of the service changes radically. I see it through their eyes, the strange code words, the unexplained movements, the dated music – Victorian or 1980s Radio 2. I want the service to communicate something of the beauty of God. It's for them.

The community

In a sense, we are there for those who are not there. We represent the wider community of people and place their interests before God. We are 'stand-ins' for those who never think of coming, but who God longs for and who the Church is there to serve.

The worship leader

If we are ordained or authorized to lead, we too are entitled to worship. We need to worship as much as anyone and we have to manage leading the worship in such a way that we too can encounter God. That's not easy but we grow into it.

Preparation

We need to think about various aspects as we prepare.

Freshly minted Those of us used to established liturgies, whether in book or onscreen, have to remember that we're not just tinkering with a set formula and only required to tinker with a few changeable items. Worship should always come across as both familiar and fresh. It should ask different things of the congregation in different weeks. We need to look at the whole service as a new opportunity. Additions and subtle changes, such as a period of silence after Communion, a poem at the start, drawing attention to the background or wording of a hymn – these small things can lift the expectancy of a congregation.

Quality Michael Mayne, former Dean of Westminster Abbey, said:

> Nothing matters more in the ordering of our churches than the quality of our worship and the care and imagination we bring to arranging the space we have to fill . . . Worship that is ill-prepared and ill-conducted and therefore 'dead theatre', or those who have lost any sense of wonder or mystery in celebrating the Eucharist and any sense of the numinous in conducting worship, are the commonest factor in emptying churches.[2]

Worship is not entertainment, but people are used to high presentation values from films, television and work settings and they expect decent quality in public performances of any kind. At the very least they expect to be warm, relatively comfortable and able to see. Imaginative lighting, colour, furnishing, hospitality and some sense of theatre are all of real importance. The American writer Annie Dillard wrote of attending a church where:

Week after week I was moved by the pitiableness of the bare linoleum-floored sacristy which no flowers could cheer or soften, by the terrible singing I so loved, by the fatigued Bible readings, the lagging emptiness and dilution of the liturgy, the horrifying vacuity of the sermon, and by the fog of dreary senselessness pervading the whole, which existed alongside, and probably caused, the wonder of the fact that we came; we returned; we showed up; week after week, we went through with it.[3]

The liturgist's report would surely say: 'Could do better.' Congregations should expect quality in their worship, whatever the style.

Musically satisfying It doesn't matter what the musical taste of the church actually is, from Sung Mass to worship band, but the music must be right for the congregation. A variety of style keeps people curious. A service that only uses Victorian hymns or an all-age service that uses the latest songs from a festival that only band members have been to are equally unhelpful to worshippers. Most responsibility is usually delegated to the musicians themselves, but clergy and leaders of worship mustn't abdicate final responsibility for seeing that worship *works*. Always remember the words of Tagore, 'God respects me when I work, but he loves me when I sing.'

The five 'S's I realize it's a personal hunch, but I think it's worth attending to the five S's when enriching worship. These are: symbol, sacrament, silence, story and song. *Symbols* often remain in the memory long after the best sermons have departed. *Sacraments* get to places other worship can't reach, places beyond rivers of words and cloudy concepts. *Silence* is a need across our entire culture, distracted and drowning as we are in noise and triviality. *Story* is the medium by which we communicate most effectively with one another from morning till night. *Song* is a plea for the use of the solo voice (live or recorded) in different ways, for example, as the service begins, for reflection after a sermon, to introduce intercessions, after receiving Communion, following the blessing. Using these 'S's takes imagination and a little risk, but the feedback from congregations is likely to be immensely positive.

Soaked in prayer We need to pray (and pray with others) about the worship we're going to lead. What are the possibilities that God is setting before us? What is unique about this Sunday with this particular congregation? What resources, old and new, do we have? How does God want us to take the worship forward? Who's involved in worship that I should be praying for in particular?

Quick idea: worship audit

Every two years or so a church might conduct a worship audit through a medium-length questionnaire for all the congregation to fill in over a four-week period (to cover all regular attenders). In this, they're asked their views on everything to do with the worship they experience in church. The questionnaire could use a scale of 'Very happy – happy – not entirely happy – unhappy' about various elements of worship, either angled to particular issues the church faces or, preferably, asking for responses on all the elements of a service of worship. There should also be room for creative thinking to be offered beyond the current norms. This would not be a referendum but, rather, valuable information for the leadership to discuss with the church council or to be the basis of a wider community conversation.

Leading worship

When we're actually leading the worship, another set of principles are important to consider.

Are we genuine? The spiritual integrity of ministers is on the line whenever they lead worship. A dutiful approach isn't enough. If I give my wife flowers saying it was my duty on our wedding anniversary and the flowers were cheap to buy, she's unlikely to be impressed. She wants my heart more than a churlish sense of duty. Isaiah wrote, 'These people . . . honour me with their lips but their hearts are far from me' (Isaiah 29.13, NIV). That mustn't be said of us as we lead worship; it has to be genuine, coming from the heart. You can tell immediately whether a priest is reading the Eucharistic Prayer or praying it. It's the same with someone leading the intercessions; are they reading their text or praying their prayers and actually addressing God? Spiritual engagement and, equally, spiritual disengagement are transparent to people with sensitivity and they want the real thing.

Are people encountering God? Our leading of worship needs to have this as a high and holy objective. It's not sufficient to go through the motions of encountering God. A South American Christian who visited Britain was asked on his return what had impressed him about the church there. He said, 'Well, all the services started punctually – even if the Spirit hadn't arrived yet.' In leading worship we're seeking an enriching encounter with the Spirit, so the way we pray, the silences we leave, the guidance we give, the careful choice of words, the space for response – all need to have that objective. Or else why should people bother to come?

Are we balancing the vertical and the horizontal? Mystery and community belong together but churches are prone to excess in one direction or the other. Some services seem lost in the mists of eternity, while others seem to be a family party with a special relative kept in the attic. Encountering God is central to worship, but we enjoy that epiphany in the good company of others, so we have to try and focus on God (at least until coffee) while rejoicing that God has given us this happy band of pilgrims as companions. There are no guidelines here; it's an art rather than a science.

Is the range of emotional engagement wide enough? Public worship often sticks with the emotional middle ground in order to relate to most people most of the time. But this can lead to a medium-strength, safety-first act of worship rather than one that climbs the star-lit stairway of joy or descends to the dark land of lament. At any time when two or three (or more) are gathered together, there will be both pleasure and pain, often unannounced and held in secret. It's worth revisiting the emotional range of the service and the way we're leading it in order to include those who are bouncing off the ceiling and those who are hanging on to their last safety rope. God has a word for them both.

How can I inhabit my God-given personality but avoid it intruding on the worship? God embodied his love in a person and he continues to do so. We aren't shadows directing worship by remote control. We are distinct personalities called by God to this ministry – don't doubt it. But this service isn't a celebrity show or a talent contest. We are enablers of worship, not the focus of it. How can we give this worship personality without that personality being the Big Me? Again, it's an art. Good luck.

Have we got the right tone for this act of worship? I suggest that the right tone is one of simple dignity. This means being neither too fussy nor too casual. I think you'll know what I mean. It's about how we move, the way we speak, how we introduce and connect the service, the phrases we use, our formality and informality. A priest at a funeral, instead of saying 'Please be seated,' said several times, 'Now have a nice sit down.' It didn't fit the occasion. Simple dignity means we recognize the privilege we've been given and try to bring a calm authority to the proceedings. That enables worshippers to find their own freedom and explore their own experience in the theatre of God.

Two last thoughts

Tom Wright says that the most common Greek word for worship in the Bible is *proskuneo*, which means, in some formulations, 'to come forward to kiss'. Lovely.

Worship isn't actually what we do at 10 a.m. on Sunday. It's how we live before God all week. It's an orientation of our whole life towards God. Sunday morning just gives us that experience in a more focused and concentrated way.

Tailpiece: the Eucharist

On his return from church one day, the actor Alec Guinness met a lapsed Catholic friend who asked him, 'Had a nice Mass?' Sir Alec wanted to reply, 'Oh, you know, the same old thing. The Real Presence at the altar, body, blood, soul, divinity of Christ, the usual.'[4]

Have we truly reckoned with the scale and seriousness of what we are doing in worship?

Resources

The possibilities here are endless. I merely note a variety of books that have been useful to me.

Jonny Baker, *Curating Worship* (London: SPCK, 2010).

Ian Bradley, *The Daily Telegraph Book of Hymns* (London: Continuum, 2005).

Paul Bradshaw (ed.), *Companion to Common Worship* (London: SPCK, 2001).

Tim Dowley, *Christian Music: A global history* (London: SPCK, 2018).

Mark Earey, *Liturgical Worship: A fresh look, how it works, why it matters* (London: Church House Publishing, 2009).

The Iona Community, *Iona Abbey Worship Book* (Glasgow: Wild Goose, 2017).

Northumbria Community, *Celtic Daily Prayer Books 1 and 2* (London: HarperCollins, 2015).

Michael Perham, *New Handbook of Pastoral Liturgy* (London: SPCK, 2000).

Bryan Spinks, *The Worship Mall: Contemporary responses to contemporary culture* (London: SPCK, 2010).

Y

Why believe? (Apologetics)

I have a great admiration for school chaplains. They're at the forefront of trying to make sense of Christian faith to young people for whom, by and large, it *doesn't* make sense. And when we have the majority of the population claiming to have no religion and a fast-falling percentage prepared to own the description 'Christian' (33 per cent in 2019), making sense of faith is clearly a major task for all Christian believers.

Of course, there are many different types of unbelief, ranging from straight atheism, through wistful agnosticism, to those who have never really thought about it. So there's no one-size-fits-all in apologetics. Understanding the question being asked is itself a complex task. Many will remember the Ronnie Barker sketch where John Cleese is asking for four candles – not to be confused with 'fork handles'.

Let's be clear about what the word apologetics means. In many ways it's an unfortunate word, suggesting back-foot defensiveness from a crumpled Christian. It's actually about commending and defending the Christian faith in a positive, creative manner. Alister McGrath helpfully writes, 'The chief goal of apologetics is to create an intelligent and imaginative climate conducive to the birth and nurture of faith.'[1]

It's important to check any instinct in ourselves that considers apologetics to be about winning a victory over another. As a young Christian I had an argument with my atheist grandmother about the resurrection. At the end she said, 'You may have won the argument, but you'll never convince me.' Grinding people down with our intellectual firepower is no way to win people for Christ. We're inviting people into a new way of seeing.

An approach

One way of marshalling our thoughts may be to look at a dinner menu of strategies in apologetics.

- Starter (testing the cuisine): what are the points of contact? Where might faith issues itch?
- Main course (the centre of the meal): argument and explanation;
- Dessert (tasty sweet course): stories and testimonies;
- Coffee (the warm finale): images;
- Wine (accompanying the whole meal): the presence of the Spirit.

Starter

In the starter, we're looking for the emotional connection that gives a reason to engage with issues of faith. If that connection isn't there, any engagement is likely to run out of road fairly quickly. In his memorable book *Unapologetic*, Francis Spufford maintains that most people who become Christians find that faith connects first with an emotional space within them that's only later backed up by argument and rationality.[2]

Now that we're living in a time when traditional Christian words and concepts are a foreign country to very many people of middle-age and younger, it's becoming increasingly important that we start farther back in our conversations about faith. We have to start with the ordinary experiences that most people have in some form or other and ask if there might be *something more* lurking within them. So, for example, there is in most of us at some stage a *sense of incompleteness*, as if we've missed out on something vital. What might that be saying? We all have the experience of *desire* and *longing*. What, ultimately, are we reaching out for? We all know what it is to feel we're in a *mess*. There's a crack in everything, but we often find that's how the light gets in. What is that light and how does it work? *Suffering* is a major reality for us all and it brings out the theologian in most of us as we ask big questions. *The arts* often leave us feeling we're on the edge of something vast. 'I tiptoe towards the deity while listening to music. Art has the power to make the universe shiver.'[3]

We're looking for common ground, believing that God is present in all things and the scent of God can be found just as much at the centre of life as at its edge. We mustn't move too swiftly from the common experience to the conviction of the believer, of course; here I'm simply wanting to illustrate that these experiences have the potential to go further and deeper, so it's a point of connection. The conversation can start here.[4]

Main course

The red meat of apologetics often lies in discussions over the existence of God, science and religion, suffering, the regressive nature of Christianity and so on. However, there may also be some more basic ground-clearing to be done. We may have to explain what Christians believe and don't believe, because some of the perceptions out there are bonkers and the areas of ignorance cavernous. Over half the population don't know what happened at Easter or are unable to give a coherent narrative of the Christmas story. Forty per cent don't think Jesus was a real person (survey, 2015).

Existence of God Early discussion might centre on different kinds of knowledge (for example, mathematical, artistic, personal) and the impossibility of Hamlet being able to prove the existence of Shakespeare. We may also have to make clear that God is not a thing among other things in the universe but, rather, the one infinite reality on which all 'things' depend for existence.

We might then be into six classic arguments for the God hypothesis being reasonable: the arguments from contemporary science (see below), from the universal sense of morality, from the experience of wonder, from the universal human instinct for the transcendent, from personal experience and from Jesus (could he be so right on everything else and so wrong on the thing on which he based his life?)

Science and religion Again, we might need early discussion about the difference between 'how questions' (mainly science) and 'why questions' (mainly religion) and about the way that different kinds of evidence are valid, not just narrowly construed scientific ones.

The main debate might then centre around four questions:

1 Why is there something rather than nothing? (the basic philosophical question);
2 Where do the 'laws' and regularities underlying the universe come from? (What is the source of rationality?);
3 Why is the universe so finely tuned to produce life? (For example, if gravity differed from its actual value by one part in ten followed by thirty-three noughts, life itself would have been impossible);
4 Why is the universe intelligible? ('The most incomprehensible thing about the universe is that it's comprehensible.' Einstein).

Suffering Discussion here requires humility and sensitivity before the universality of suffering and the profound effect it has on everyone, including the people we're talking to at the time. It may help to establish that there are different levels of discussion, dependent on who we're talking to, where and when. We might be responding on an emotional/pastoral, faith/spiritual or philosophical/intellectual level and the conversations will be very different indeed (see **Suffering**).

However, there is something to be said that represents the beginnings – of an approach – of a first shot – at making a guess – at the ways of God in a world of accident and pain. This isn't to minimise the horror, but merely to offer a framework through which we can see that, in spite of everything, this is still 'the best of all possible worlds'.

The regressive record of Christianity We accept the facts, with honesty and regret. But in defence we could argue the following.

1 Any good thing can become unhealthy if it's twisted far enough (food, sex, ambition, sport, self-defence and so on). Christians try to keep to the original and best of the 'good thing' of faith, guided by what Jesus actually taught and practised.
2 Violence is often mislabelled as religious when in fact it's political and tribal, using religion as a convenient badge.
3 Huge good, of infinite benefit to humankind, has been done and is done daily by people of faith.

These and other big topics will form the basis of the Main Course of apologetic engagement, but we should beware the gridlock of sterile argument. Something more fundamental needs to change than mere mental constructs. (This may be where the wine of the Spirit comes in.)

Dessert

This is the tasty sweet course of stories and personal testimony. It lightens and humanizes the heavy main course of argument. We live in a story-soaked culture that envelops us in stories from the moment we get up. There's no news without a story; nothing sells without a story; television, film and novels are story-based; social media depend on millions of mini-stories every day. And all the time we have the greatest story of all.

At the end of the book and film *Life of Pi*, the hero tells a second, more conventional story to the bewildered agents of an insurance company who are unconvinced by the first story of his astonishing travels in a small boat with a Bengal tiger. Lying in his hospital bed Pi asks them, 'Which story do you prefer?'[5] It's the basic apologetic question. Do people prefer the God story or the non-God story? Which story makes more sense?

We have a million God-stories to tell if we can gather them from centuries of Christian experience and millions of Christian lives across the world. If we're called to preach or give talks there's great value in collecting these stories, quotes, images and ideas as you come across them. They appear on the Internet, in newspapers, books and magazines. They're told us by friends, heard in talks and sermons, seen in films and noticed in the street. I have an invaluable collection of thousands of such stories and quotes, collected over the years and written or pasted on to file cards (clunky but effective). In the event of a house fire, after the family, they're the first things that I would rescue!

There's usually a very positive response to having a celebrity alumnus, an athlete, an explorer or a television personality turn up at a school to give a talk. The same principle is at work when we have Christians of the famous or 'locally sourced' variety speaking of their own faith. It's the power of personal story. Indeed, if Christians all over the country could be persuaded to loosen up and tell their faith story, in whole or in part, a powerful wave of evangelism would be released. All we are trying to do is to bring the Christian story alongside people's own story so that they can interact. The rest is up to God.

Coffee

I want to put in a word for images as the warm finale to the apologetic meal. Our minds are more like art galleries than libraries; they retain images more than concepts. You can grasp a good image, work with it, live in it and adapt it. Jesus did it all the time; look at his parables about seeds, wheat and weeds, productive and unproductive vines, specks of wood, camels and needles and so on. Sometimes he developed the image into a story; sometimes he left them as images. In the series of talks I'm doing at present in a religious community, I've used images such as streams pouring down a mountainside, a house with rooms that have no windows, a glorious river pouring past a dry river-bank, a set of images of Jesus and so on. I guarantee they'll lodge in the mind longer than some of the straight teaching. They work at the level of instinct and so bypass the slower analytical processes of argument.

Quick idea: Apologetics Café

The questions are all out there, as much inside the Church as outside. An Apologetics Café is an opportunity to address some of them without it being too threatening. There's a more church-based and a more secular model of this. The former could be an event at a normal Café Church; the latter at a friendly coffee shop. Participants sit around their tables with coffee and cake and can either write their own questions or choose from a set of cards of common, tough questions. One, two or three people who might be expected to be able to tackle the questions then collect them and, with a proactive chairperson, do their best to give some answers and generate discussion. It's bound to be stimulating and, hopefully, genuinely helpful. Having more than one person means both that different expertise is available and that sometimes different angles on the same question can emerge. There are, after all, no perfect answers.

Wine

Wine creates an agreeable atmosphere in which the meal and accompanying conversation take place. In apologetics, without the 'lubricating' work of the Holy Spirit, nothing significant will happen. The Spirit is the interpreter, the go-between, the gentle persuader. We need to pray about our apologetic opportunities, whether they be in schools, pubs, coffee shops, beginners' groups, at work, the school gate or wherever. As always, we are only joining in with what the Holy Spirit is doing in the minds and hearts of people who have a potential interest in faith, but our conversation gives God the space and opportunity to do that work. The Holy Spirit needs us; we need the Holy Spirit.

Tailpiece: a science professor remembers

The attitude that science and religion are incompatible is not new. I first met it fifty years ago while studying at Cambridge. I found myself at a formal dinner sitting beside a Nobel Prize winner. I tried to ask him some questions. For instance, how did his science shape his world-view? I was interested in whether his studies had led him to reflect on the existence of God. It was clear he wasn't comfortable with that question and I backed off. However, at the end of the meal he invited me to come to his study with two or three other senior academics. I was invited to sit; they stood. He said, 'Lennox, do you want a career in science?' 'Yes sir,' I replied. 'Then you must give up this childish faith in God. If you don't it will cripple you intellectually. You simply will not make it.' I sat in the chair, shocked by the effrontery and unexpectedness of the onslaught.

Eventually I managed to blurt out, 'Sir, what have you got to offer me that is better than what I've got?' He said, 'Creative evolution.' I couldn't see how this philosophy was enough to provide a foundation for meaning, morality and life. I told the group standing around me that I found the biblical world-view vastly more enriching and the evidence for its truth compelling and so, with all due respect, I would take the risk and stick with it. Here was a brilliant scientist trying to bully me into giving up Christianity. If it had been the other way around, and I had been an atheist in the chair surrounded by Christian academics pressurising me, it would probably have ended up with disciplinary proceedings against the professors involved. But that scary incident put steel in my heart and mind. I resolved to be as good a scientist as I could be and to encourage people to think about the big questions of God and science and to make up their own minds without being bullied or pressured.[6]

Resources

Andy Bannister, *The Atheist Who Didn't Exist: Or the dreadful consequences of bad argument* (Oxford: Lion Hudson, 2015).

Justin Brieley, *Unbelievable: Why after ten years of talking with atheists, I'm still a Christian* (London: SPCK, 2017).

Michael Green, *Lies, Lies, Lies: Exposing myths about the real Jesus* (Nottingham: IVP, 2009).

Timothy Keller, *The Reason for God: Belief in an age of scepticism* (London: Hodder & Stoughton, 2009).

John Lennox, *Can Science Explain Everything?* (Epsom, Surrey: The Good Book Company, 2019).

Alister McGrath, *Mere Apologetics: How to help seekers and sceptics find faith* (London: SPCK, 2016).

Tim Muehlhoff and Richard Langer, *Winsome Persuasion: Christian influence in a post-Christian world* (Downers Grove, IL: IVP Academic, 2017).

John Pritchard, *How to Explain Your Faith* (London: SPCK, 2014).

Francis Spufford, *Unapologetic* (London: Faber and Faber, 2012).

Y

Young people

Race for Jesus

When I was a Diocesan Youth Officer talking to youth workers, I often started with two quotes. One came from Shakespeare's *Winter's Tale*, 'I would that there were no age between sixteen and three and twenty, or that youth would sleep out the rest; for there is nothing in between but getting wenches with child, wronging the ancientry, stealing and fighting.' It's still a popular view among bewildered adults.

I also asked these youth workers if they had any idea when and where the following might have been written, 'This youth is rotten from the bottom of their hearts. The young people are malicious and lazy; they will never be as young people were before. Our today's youth will not be able to maintain our culture.' Any guesses? The answer is it was found in the ruins of old Babylon and dated three thousand years ago.

The fact is that young people have incredible reserves of energy, are programmed to be untidy, suddenly need inordinate amounts of sleep, are addicted to social media, cost a fortune, love their pets more than they love their parents and are deeply insecure. But they're idealistic, creative, fun, have a great capacity for love and loyalty, want to make a difference to the world and long for a steady, loving environment to grow up in.

The problem

The local church used to be one of the main providers of youth work across the nation. Now half of Anglican churches have in their congregation fewer than five children and young people under the age of sixteen. We know that by their early twenties the great majority of young people will have made their basic decisions about their world-view, the nexus of values, priorities and beliefs that shape their future actions. This is the age when most adult Christians will have come to faith. Indeed, some research claims that eighty per cent of adult Christians found their faith before they were twenty-one. If we miss this crucial age, we'll have a much harder task later on.

Let's not rehearse the reasons why the Church has such a low approval rating from young people – it's too depressing. Let's focus on the principles that make for effective work among young people. But first, it's important to try and grasp how differently Generation Z (those born between 1995 and 2012) approach their culture and context.[1]

- *A broken and fragile world* Gen Z live in a post-9/11 world marked by financial crashes, a cascade of global terrorism and apparently imminent climate catastrophe. They're cynical about political leaders but idealistic about reinventing how the world works. And they're out on the streets, connecting and collaborating in new ways.
- *Wi-fi enabled* Gen Z have never known a time without smartphones and they spend huge amounts of the day consuming media (YouTube, social media, TV/film). While older generations might criticize this obsession, Gen Z do their connecting digitally and form relationships this way. Separation from a smartphone causes real anxiety because it's like switching off reality.
- *Visual* Gen Z language is rooted in short videos, vlogs, Snapchat and emojis. Hour-long services where you sit in

rows, face the front, sing strange hymns and listen to long sermons, don't help them. For them, being in such a situation is like being in a foreign country.

- *Sexually fluid* Tolerance is the ultimate value. Inclusivity, diversity and equality are the ideals that have shaped Gen Z and they're uncomfortable with labels about sexual orientation. There's a common belief that individual sexuality should be expressed as and when it's felt to be appropriate.
- *Post Christian* Gen Z is the first truly post-Christian generation, brought up by non-Christian parents. The level of ignorance of the Christian story is amazing to earlier, church-going generations but Gen Z shouldn't be blamed. It's the way it is. 'Atheist' is no longer a dirty word.

So this is where we're starting from, but it should be remembered that this 'clean sheet' about Christianity is also an opportunity where younger people may be free of hang-ups about the faith and open to explore. They take things on their merits. This is primary mission, as demanding as it's ever been.

Background tools

Although the situation is serious and the need to take action is urgent, it's important not simply to jump on the latest 'new thing' to try and reconnect with young people. Some background understanding of educational psychology will help us to find out which are the best actions to take in the long run.

1 Faith development theory

James Fowler is one among several educationalists who have proposed faith development theories to help us understand the processes going on in the life of faith. He suggests the following, although the descriptors are mine.[2]

Foundational faith (0–4 years old) Essentially pre-images of God mediated through love.

Unordered faith (4–8) Made up of a collage of images and beliefs from a child's imagination, received stories and experiences of the world.

Ordered faith (7–12) The great era of story as experience is given shape by the child and more concrete images emerge from the previous kaleidoscope.

Conformist faith (12–18) A more reflective faith but formed by drawing together disparate elements and a desire to fit in with others.

Chosen faith (18+ or late 30s+) A personal faith but in danger of oversimplification and binary thinking, needing tidiness and certainty.

Both/and faith (rare before 30) More open, inclusive and accepting of paradox, seeking understanding rather than explanation. Symbol, myth and story speak again.

Universalizing faith (only in later life and rare) The self is relinquished, the whole human race is embraced in love. Only 0.3 per cent of Fowler's research interviewees were in this group.

This scheme isn't meant to be a set of cages in which to trap people, but an indicator of a process that can stop at any point, be repeated or go in a spiral. It's a helpful background to our work with young people – and adults too.

2 Dynamic/learning cycle

This is a well-established process in informal education. It's how we learn (and in particular here, how young people learn) when offered an inductive, experience-based approach. Very simply, it looks like the diagram on the next page.

1 Experience   4 Further action

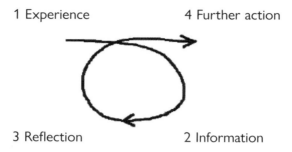

3 Reflection   2 Information

Experience Young people see a film, do a night hike, meet an interesting Christian, do a litter-pick, take flowers to visit people in a care home and so on.

Information Back at base they report on the experience and are offered relevant information on the subject of the film, environmental factors about the walk, the interesting Christian's hidden profile, the scale of the problem of litter and the crisis in social care.

Reflection The leaders introduce some Christian themes that relate to the experience and the young people's understanding of it, enriched now with new information. The Bible, theology, Christian biography, ethics and spirituality all become relevant.

Further action The 'so what?' stage. What would we do differently now we've been through the cycle of learning? How can we now respond afresh?

3 Learning styles
See **Teaching.**

Basic principles
Everyone involved in youth work has their own favourite basic principles. These are mine.

- *Youth ministry must be church-wide, not a separate entity* Young people enjoy connectedness, being accepted and valued by the whole congregation and this makes for a much more effective ministry. This commitment from the wider church should show itself in the church budget, by older people taking opportunities to talk to younger ones, by adults supporting youth activities more. It's worth noting here too that the image of a young trendy youth worker is too easily invoked as the ideal. One of the most successful youth workers in a diocese where I worked was in her sixties and had total loyalty from her teenage bikers.

- *The church must be authentic in practising what it preaches* Young people can sniff out a fraud at a hundred metres and if the church preaches about care for the poor and marginalized, it will have to show it in its work with the homeless, the foodbank, asylum seekers and other social concerns. Practical social justice is important to young people and they want to see the church walk the talk.

- *Go for genuineness over flair* It's easy to think that young people want smart, high-quality, exciting events, but they are more likely to value substance over sparkle. They usually prefer to be taken seriously, given a warm welcome and offered love and support. The motto could be 'don't be cool; be warm.'

- *Always consider issues of participation and empowerment* Young people are not just the recipients of adults' wisdom and bounty. They need and want to participate in different ways to the whole life of the church, to be on working groups, on the church council when they're legally old enough; they need to be let loose in worship and encouraged and enabled to take on their own social outreach. Above all, they need to be listened to and taken seriously as members of today's church as well as offering hope for tomorrow.

> ### Quick idea: consultation
>
> Don't do anything without having called together, over pizza, all the young people who might be interested in some kind of activity and asking them what they might like to do. It sounds obvious, but it's a crucial first stage that both takes the teenagers seriously and gets an accurate picture of where they really are rather than one dreamed up in an adult's imagination. And be realistic – if all they want at first is a trip to a movie and more pizza, so be it. Then you can suggest something more.

What helps young people to grow in faith?

Family nurture

Nothing helps more than a good experience of a family living out its Christian commitment naturally, unselfconsciously and confidently. Young people are greatly helped by open conversation that tackles significant issues they're running into and that doesn't run away from doubt. Young people need to be respected in their discoveries about life – and in their decisions about going to church.

Other significant adults

So often you hear in later life that it was the example of a minister, youth worker, teacher or other adult in the church that impressed the person when they were young. These relationships can't be fixed or contrived but they can be encouraged and celebrated.

Peak experiences

It's a great boon if young people have an experience outside the normal run of activity that shows them that the Christian faith can be exciting, profound and relevant to their growing lives. This could be at a summer youth festival, Lee Abbey, Taizé,

Walsingham or any number of other venues. If the church could offer small bursaries, it would demonstrate an important commitment to the nurture of young people and send a welcome signal. Again, in later life an adult Christian will often point to some such event as being truly significant in them finding their own faith. At the last Soul Survivor events in 2019, over two thousand young people made Christian commitments.

Peer group

Teen age is a time of peer-group support as well as pressure. Lively Christian youth groups in churches are increasingly rare but school groups sometimes deputize for them or else there can be groups of friends who meet at one event and decide to keep in touch through social media. Solitary young Christians can be very exposed among their sceptical peers, so any means of grouping them together should be used. There are often more teenagers around a church than we realize when choir, worship band, bell-ringers, servers, confirmation candidates and others are taken into account.

Social action

Teenagers are idealistic when properly engaged. Projects that benefit the environment or support elderly people, offbeat money-raising activities for charities or sprucing up a community building – all such things can find teenagers happily enlisting. Even more significant can be mission trips abroad where a group goes to help paint a school or build a church or work in an orphanage. These trips can be life changing.

Mentoring

An adult taking a young person under his or her wing has proved time and again to be one of the most helpful ways of encouraging an emerging faith. Best of all (though rare) would be someone in their twenties mentoring a teenager before memories have got too distant. Questions, reading the Bible together, talking about life and its pressures can form the 'syllabus'. Of course, we have to be very aware of safeguarding issues and the church safeguarding officer should advise.

Contemplative youth ministry

That's the name of an excellent book by Mark Yaconelli[3] in which he argues and demonstrates that many young people respond much more to approaches that utilize ancient spiritual disciplines in modern form than to all-action, zappy but rather trivial programmes. For example, the Jesuit Examen is a classic way of reflection on God's presence in everyday life over the last day or week. Lectio divina is an ancient way of feeding deeply on Scripture rather than galloping superficially through familiar stories. Stillness and symbolic actions can communicate profoundly to young people saturated with noise, text, image and advert. These more contemplative approaches to youth work are embedding serious spiritual practices into young hearts and they show that Christian faith has depth.

Encountering Jesus and the Big Bible Story

The key word is 'encounter'. A living experience is worth a hundred Christian talks. As above with contemplative youth ministry, the goal of Christian youth work should be that young people, in freedom and without pressure, will encounter God and find in God a rock on which to build their lives. Ignorance of the Big Bible Story, even in Christian families, is at record levels, so interesting ways of getting hold of the big picture are important. There are lots of aids to this, but one of the best is to move the group around a large space as you tell the story from Abraham to St Paul. Detail isn't required, but the physical act of moving around embeds the story in muscle memory while being enjoyable and fun.

Essentials

This is a 'quick-fire round' of essential elements of youth work. Maybe you can do better.

A: Activity – a balance of the physical and the cerebral
B: Boundaries – just so they know
C: Comfort – sofas and big chairs, sympathetic lighting
D: Democracy – shared ownership of the group
E: Enthusiasm – it attracts
F: Food – any sort, in quantity
G: Generosity – an introduction to grace
H: Happiness – balanced with seriousness, even sadness
I: Identity – teenagers' basic search
J: Justice, social – catch the group's enthusiasms
K: Killing – not allowed
L: Laughter – self-generating if all is going well
M: Music – their choice
N: Nurture – the goal of youth work
O: Openness – no off-the-peg answers
P: Parents – off limits unless expressly invited to some event
R: Relationships – it's all about this
S: Stories – basic raw material
T: Testimony – always powerful
U: University – they go too soon
V: Value – what is the added value this youth work brings?
W: Worship – let them develop their own
X: X Factor – surprises are enjoyable
Y: Yes – say it much more than no
Z: Zoo – go there if all else fails

Tailpiece: a young person following Jesus

A youth minister, a committed Christian, called one evening after receiving a phone call from her college-age son. She sounded distressed as she told me [Mark Yaconelli] that her son had decided to leave his studies in order to join a group of Americans who were going to Iraq to be with Iraqi citizens during the American bombing and occupation. The hope was that by being a visible presence as American citizens they might be able to protect the lives of civilians as well as increase awareness about the suffering of Iraqis back in the US. My friend was upset and told her son that he had made a commitment to college and that this was no time to engage in radical politics. I asked her how her son responded. She sighed; there was quiet over the phone line for a moment. Then she said with tears in her voice, 'He said, "But Mom, this isn't politics. This is about following Jesus. We're going as a Christian group. Didn't you and the church teach me that Jesus was always befriending people who were weak and suffering?"' I waited in silence. I could hear her crying. Then finally she said, 'He's right you know. I know he's right. But if I knew he was going to do something like this I would have taken him out of the church and raised him to be a Chippendale dancer.'[4]

Discuss.

Resources

CPAS, 'Growing Leaders: Youth Edition' (www.cpas.org.uk/church-resources/growing-leaders-suite/growing-leaders-youth-edition#.XmU6AS2cZTY>).

Premier (<www.youthandchildrens.work>).

Nick Shepherd, *Faith Generation: Retaining young people and growing the Church* (London: SPCK, 2016).

Y Young people

Miranda Threlfall-Holmes, *The Teenage Prayer Experiment Notebook* (London: SPCK, 2015).

Mark Yaconelli, *Contemplative Youth Ministry: Practising the presence of Jesus with young people* (London: SPCK, 2014).

Youth For Christ (<https://resources.yfc.co.uk>).

Youth Work Resource (<www.youthworkresource.com>).

Z

Or rather Zzzzzzzzzzzz

I hope you get enough of it. We have to be disciplined about not filling every waking hour or 'just slipping into the study'.

Charles Schulz, the Snoopy cartoonist, had a character say, 'Sometimes I lie awake at night and I ask, "Where have I gone wrong?" Then a voice says to me, "This is going to take more than one night."'

If you have that experience, don't entertain it.

Go back to sleep.

Notes

A word at the beginning

1 John Pritchard, *The Life and Work of a Priest* (London: SPCK, 2007).
2 Martyn Percy (ed.), *The Study of Ministry: A comprehensive survey of theory and best practice* (London: SPCK, 2019).
3 Brian McLaren, *The Great Spiritual Migration: How the world's largest religion is seeking a better way to be Christian* (Danvers, MA: Convergent, 2016), p. 2.

Attentiveness

1 St John of the Cross, *The Living Flame of Love* (London: SPCK, 2017).
2 Kosuke Koyama, *Three Mile an Hour God: Biblical reflections* (New York: Orbis, 1979), pp. 6–7.
3 Simone Weil, quoted in *The Week*, 10 December 2016, originally from a letter to her friend and poet Joë Bousquet, 13 April 1942.
4 Barbara Brown Taylor, *An Altar in the World: Finding the sacred beneath our feet* (New York: HarperOne, 2009), p. 109.

Bible

1 Quoted by Nick Page in *God's Dangerous Book* (Milton Keynes: Authentic Media, 2011), introduction.
2 Rowan Williams, *Being Christian: Baptism, Bible, Eucharist, prayer* (London: SPCK, 2014), p. 24.
3 A. N. Wilson, *The Book of the People: How to read the Bible* (London: Atlantic Books, 2015), p. 191.

Care and compassion

1 Taken from David Nott, *War Doctor: Surgery on the front line* (London: Pan Macmillan, 2019).
2 Pierre Teilhard de Chardin, 'The evolution of chastity', in *Toward the Future*, translated by René Hague (1973), as quoted in *Seed Sown: Theme and reflections on the Sunday lectionary reading (Cycles A, B, and C)* by Jay Cormier (New York: Sheed & Ward, 1996), p. 33.
3 Julian the Apostate, letter to Arsacius (AD 362), in *The Works of the Emperor Julian*, Vol. 3, Loeb Classical Library (1913).
4 Thomas Merton, *The Hidden Ground of Love: Letters* (London: Macmillan, 1985/2011).

Children and schools

1 William Wordsworth, *Ode: Intimations of Immortality from Recollections of Early Childhood* in *Poems in Two Volumes* (1807).

2 Fynn, *Mister God, This is Anna* (London: HarperCollins, 1974), p. 36.

Death

1 Julian Barnes, *Nothing to be Frightened of* (London: Vintage, 2009), p. 70.

2 Bertrand Russell, *Autobiography, Vol. 2* (London: Allen & Unwin, 1968), p. 159.

3 Terry Ryan, *The Prize Winner of Defiance: How my mother raised kids on 25 words or less* (New York: Simon & Schuster, 2001).

4 Dietrich Bonhoeffer, *Letters and Papers from Prison* (London: SCM Press, 2013).

5 Denise Inge, *A Tour of Bones: Facing fear and looking for life* (London: Bloomsbury, 2014).

6 Adapted from Mark Yaconelli, *Disappointment, Doubt and Other Spiritual Gifts: Reflections on life and ministry* (London: SPCK, 2016), p. 133.

Evangelism

1 In an interview at St Mellitus theological training conference, 2 December, 2013.

2 Dietrich Bonhoeffer, *The Cost of Discipleship* (London: SCM Press, 1948/2001), p. 44.

3 Brian McLaren, *More Ready Than You Realize: The power of everyday conversations* (Grand Rapids, MI: Zondervan, 2002), p. 146

Forgiveness

1 Sam Hailes, 'Moby: How a skinny, teetotal vegan DJ with a Christian faith conquered dance music', *Premier Christianity*, April, 2017 (available online at: <www.premierchristianity.com/Past-Issues/2017/April-2017>).

2 The story is told in Terri Roberts, *Forgiven: The Amish school shooting* (Grand Rapids, MI: Bethany House Publishers, 2015).

3 'Is it always better to forgive?', *The Times*, 8 March 2006 (available online at: <www.thetimes.co.uk/article/is-it-always-better-to-forgive-dshnwtj63dj>).

4 *The Times*, 8 March.

5 Brother Alois, Prior of Taizé, at the 33rd European Meeting, Rotterdam, 2011.

6 'Times 2', *The Times*, February, 2005.

God

1 Douglas Coupland, *Life after God* (New York: Pocket Books, 1958), p. 359.
2 Richard Dawkins, *The God Delusion* (London: Bantam Press, 2006), p.31.
3 Mark Oakley, *The Splash of Words; Believing in poetry* (Norwich: Canterbury Press, 2016), p. 24.
4 Elise Fletcher, 'Urban neighbours of hope', *Church Times*, 22 June, 2018.

Holy Communion

1 Gregory Dix, *The Shape of the Liturgy* (London: Dacre Press, 1945).
2 Eucharistic Prayer G, *Common Worship* (London: Church House Publishing, 2000).
3 Rowan Williams, *Being Christian: Baptism, Bible, Eucharist, prayer* (London: SPCK, 2014), p. 53.
4 Timothy Radcliffe, *Seven Last Words* (London: Burns & Oates, 2004), p. 44.
5 Harry Williams, *Jesus and the Resurrection* (London: Longmans, 1952), p. 19.
6 *Book of Common Prayer*, 'Solemnization of matrimony'.
7 Source not found.

Jesus

1 Michael Mayne, *Responding to the Light: Reflections on Advent, Christmas and Epiphany* (Norwich: Canterbury Press, 2017), p. 6.
2 Seen on a poster in Hamilton, New Zealand.
3 Justin Welby in an interview at New Wine, 29 July, 2013.

Kingdom of God

1 Bishop Michael Curry, from his sermon for the wedding of Prince Harry and Meghan Markle, 2018.
2 In James Bratt (ed.), *Abraham Kuyper: A centennial reader* (Grand Rapids, MI: Eerdmans, 1998), p. 461.
3 Belden Lane, *The Solace of Fierce Landscapes: Exploring desert and mountain spirituality* (Oxford: Oxford University Press, 1998), p. 219, note 5.
4 Mike Riddell, *Sacred Journey: Spiritual wisdom for times of transition* (Oxford: Lion, 2000), p. 90.

Leadership

1 Rule of St Benedict 64: 11, 12, 15, 19.

Narrative

1 Mark Oakley, *By Way of the Heart: The seasons of faith* (Norwich: Canterbury Press, 2019), p. 159.
2 James Bryan Smith, *The Good and Beautiful God: Falling in love with the God Jesus knows* (London: Hodder & Stoughton, 2011), p. 265.
3 Neil MacGregor, quoted in Andy Frost, *Long Story Short: Finding your place in God's unfolding story* (London: SPCK, 2018), p. 55.
4 James Hopewell, *Congregation: Stories and structures* (London: SCM Press, 1988).
5 Yiannis Gabriel, 'Narrative ecologies and the role of counter-narratives', in S. Frandsen, T. Kuhn and M. Wolff Lundholt (eds), *Counter-narratives and Organization* (Abingdon: Routledge, 2016), p. 208–26.

Older people

1 Age UK, 'Later life in the UK, 2019' (available online at: <www.ageuk.uk/globalassets/age-uk/documents/reports-and-publications/later_life_uk_factsheet.pdf>).

Prayer

1 Aaron Niequist, *The Eternal Current: How a practice-based faith can save us from drowning* (New York: Waterbrook, 2018).

Preaching

1 *The Times*, 10 October 1998.
2 Carmine Gallo, *Talk Like Ted* (London: Pan Macmillan, 2014), p. 8.
3 Andy Stanley and Lane Jones, *Communicating for a Change: Seven keys to irresistible communication* (Colorado Springs, CO: Multnomah Press, 2006)
4 Eugene L. Lowry, *The Homiletical Plot: The sermon as narrative art form* (Atlanta, GA: John Knox, 1980).

Questions

1 Goethe, quoted in M. Arditti, *Jubilate* (Arcadia Books, 2011), epigraph.
2 Rowan Williams, *Being Disciples: Essentials of the Christian life* (London: SPCK, 2016), p. 72.

Renewal

1 Lucy Winkett, *Our Sound is our Wound: Contemplative listening to a noisy world* (London: Continuum, 2010), p. 32.
2 Nadia Bolz-Weber, *Accidental Saints: Finding God in all the wrong people* (Norwich: Canterbury Press, 2015), p. 178.

3 Gerard Hughes SJ, *God of Surprises* (Darton, Longman & Todd, 2008).

4 See Sean Stillman, *God's Biker: Motorcycles and misfits* (London: SPCK, 2020).

5 'Philip Pullman faces his daemons' *Times Online*, 17 March 2009 (available online at: <www.thetimes.co.uk/article/philip-pullman-faces-his-daemons-ptfbtj2vrvd>).

6 Barbara Brown Taylor, *Leaving Church: A memoir of faith* (Norwich: Canterbury Press, 2011), p. 221.

7 Christina Patterson, 'Thank God for the Church of England', *The Independent*, 25 July, 2009.

Self-care

1 Dr Eve Poole, 'How to break free from a culture of overwork', *Church Times*, 18 October, 2019.

Suffering

1 Alan Hargrave, *One for Sorrow: A memoir of death and life* (London: SPCK, 2017) p. 25.

2 Michael Rosen, *We're Going on a Bear Hunt* (Walker Books, 1989).

3 Stephen Fry, *The Meaning of Life*, RTE Television, 1 February, 2015.

4 Elie Wiesel, *Night* (London: Penguin, 2008).

5 David Hume, *Dialogues Concerning Natural Religion* (1779).

6 John V. Taylor, *The Christ-Like God* (London: SCM Press, 1992), p.196.

7 Verse of a hymn by Isaac Watts, 'When I survey the wondrous cross', in *Hymns and Spiritual Songs*, 1707.

8 Kate Bowler, *Everything Happens for a Reason and Other Lies I Have Loved* (London: SPCK, 2019), p. 121.

Unity

1 Mark Oakley, *By Way of the Heart: The seasons of faith* (Norwich: Canterbury Press, 2019), p. 52.

2 Rowan Williams, *Silence and Honey Cakes: The wisdom of the desert* (Oxford: Lion, 2003), p.110.

Worship

1 Thomas Merton, *The Seven Storey Mountain* (London: SPCK, 2009).

2 Michael Mayne, *Pray, Love, Remember* (London: Darton, Longman & Todd, 1998), p.107.

3 Annie Dillard, *Teaching a Stone to Talk* (London: Canongate, 2017).

4 Alec Guinness, *A Commonplace Book* (London: Hamish Hamilton, 2001).

Why believe? (Apologetics)

1 Alister McGrath, *Bridgebuilding: Communicating Christianity effectively* (Nottingham: IVP, 1992).

2 Francis Spufford, *Unapologetic* (London: Faber and Faber, 2012).

3 Bel Mooney, *Devout Sceptics: Conversations on faith and doubt* (London: BBC Books, 2003), p. 7.

4 This common ground is explored in John Pritchard, *Something More: Encountering the beyond in the everyday* (London: SPCK, 2016).

5 Yann Martel, *Life of Pi* (London: Canongate, 2002).

6 John Lennox, Emeritus Professor of Mathematics at the University of Oxford, in *Christianity* magazine, July, 2019 (see also: <www.thegoodbook.co.uk/blog/interestingthoughts/2019/01/09/the-time-john-lennox-was-pressured-to-give-up-his-/>).

Young people

1 The material here owes much to an article by Tim Alford in *Christianity* magazine, October, 2019, p. 44 (available online at: <www.premierchristianity.com/Past-Issues/2019/October-2019/What-every-Christian-needs-to-know-about-Generation-Z>).

2 A helpful discussion of Fowler and faith development theories is found in *How Faith Grows: Faith development and Christian education* (London: National Society and Church House Publishing, 1991).

3 Mark Yaconelli, *Contemplative Youth Ministry: Practising the presence of Jesus with young people* (London: SPCK, 2014).

4 Mark Yaconelli, *Contemplative Youth Ministry*.

WE HAVE A VISION
OF A WORLD IN
WHICH EVERYONE IS
TRANSFORMED BY
CHRISTIAN KNOWLEDGE

As well as being an award-winning publisher, SPCK is the oldest Anglican mission agency in the world.

Our mission is to lead the way in creating books and resources that help everyone to make sense of faith.

Will you partner with us to put good books into the hands of prisoners, great assemblies in front of schoolchildren and reach out to people who have not yet been touched by the Christian faith?

To donate, please visit www.spckpublishing.co.uk/donate or call our friendly fundraising team on 020 7592 3900.